Choosing Health High School

ABSTINENCE

Jeanie M. White, EdM, CHES
Nancy Abbey

ETR Associates
Santa Cruz, California
1997

ETR Associates (Education, Training and Research) is a nonprofit organization committed to fostering the health, well-being and cultural diversity of individuals, families, schools and communities. The publishing program of ETR Associates provides books and materials that empower young people and adults with the skills to make positive health choices. We invite health professionals to learn more about our high-quality publishing, training and research programs by contacting us at P.O. Box 1830, Santa Cruz, CA 95061-1830, (800) 321-4407.

Jeanie M. White, EdM, CHES, is a Certified Health Education Specialist with experience teaching at all levels. She has been involved in health education in a variety of ways over the past 25 years, in both corporate and public positions. She currently works as a consultant specializing in curriculum, methods and comprehensive school health programs.

Nancy Abbey, director of training at ETR Associates, is a nationally known sexuality educator with 25 years experience as a trainer and program manager in family life education, including 18 years as a classroom teacher. She has worked extensively with parents, teachers, teens, clergy and community agencies on various family life education projects, and has developed trainings and curricula on numerous topics, including multicultural issues, substance abuse prevention and abstinence education.

Choosing Health High School

- Abstinence
- Body Image and Eating Disorders
- Communication and Self-Esteem
- Fitness and Health
- STD and HIV
- Sexuality and Relationships
- Tobacco, Alcohol and Drugs
- Violence and Injury

Series Editor: Kathleen Middleton, MS, CHES
Text design: Graphic Elements
Illustrations: Ann Smiley

 Published by ETR Associates,
P.O. Box 1830, Santa Cruz, CA 95061-1830

Printed in the United States of America

10 9 8 7 6 5 4 3 2 1
ISBN 1-56071-525-1

Title No. H687

Contents

Contents

Contents

Contents

Masters

Contents

Acknowledgments

Choosing Health High School was made possible with the assistance of dedicated curriculum developers, teachers and health professionals. This program evolved from *Entering Adulthood*, the high school component of the *Contemporary Health Series*. The richness of this new program is demonstrated by the pool of talented professionals involved in both the original and the new versions.

Developers

Nancy Abbey
ETR Associates
Santa Cruz, California

Clint E. Bruess, EdD, CHES
University of Alabama at Birmingham
Birmingham, Alabama

Dale W. Evans, HSD, CHES
California State University, Long Beach
Long Beach, California

Susan C. Giarratano, EdD, CHES
California State University, Long Beach
Long Beach, California

Betty M. Hubbard, EdD, CHES
University of Central Arkansas
Conway, Arkansas

Lisa K. Hunter, PhD
Health & Education Communication Consultants
Berkeley, California

Susan J. Laing, MS, CHES
Department of Veterans Affairs Medical Center
Birmingham, Alabama

Donna Lloyd-Kolkin, PhD
Health & Education Communication Consultants
New Hope, Pennsylvania

Jeanie M. White, EdM, CHES
Education Consultant
Keizer, Oregon

Reviewers and Consultants

Brian Adams
Family Planning Council of Western Massachusetts
Northampton, Massachusetts

Janel Siebern Bartlett, MS, CHES
Dutchess County BOCES
Poughkeepsie, NY

Lori J. Bechtel, PhD
Pennsylvania State University, Altoona Campus
Altoona, Pennsylvania

Judith M. Boswell, RN, MS, CHES
University of New Mexico
Albuquerque, New Mexico

Marika Botha, PhD
Lewis and Clark State College
Lewiston, Idaho

Wanda Bunting
Newark Unified School District
Newark, California

John Daniels
Golden Sierra High School
Garden Valley, California

Joyce V. Fetro, PhD, CHES
San Francisco Unified School District
San Francisco, California

Mark L. Giese, EdD, FACSM
Northeastern State University
Tahlequah, Oklahoma

Karen Hart, MS, CHES
San Francisco Unified School District
San Francisco, California

Janet L. Henke
Old Court Middle School
Randallstown, Maryland

Russell G. Henke, MEd
Montgomery County Public Schools
Rockville, Maryland

Jon W. Hisgen, MS
Pewaukee Public Schools
Waukesha, Wisconsin

Bob Kampa
Gilroy High School
Gilroy, California

Freya Klein Kaufmann, MS, CHES
New York Academy of Medicine
New York, New York

David M. Macrina, PhD
University of Alabama at Birmingham
Birmingham, Alabama

Linda D. McDaniel, MS
Van Buren Middle School
Van Buren, Arkansas

Robert McDermott, PhD
University of South Florida
Tampa, Florida

Acknowledgments

Carole McPherson, MA
Mentor Teacher Mission Hill Junior High School
Santa Cruz, California

Robert Mischell, MD
University of California, Berkeley
Berkeley, California

Donna Muto, MS
Mount Ararat School
Topsham, Maine

Priscilla Naworski, MS, CHES
California Department of Education
Healthy Kids Resource Center
Alameda County Office of Education
Alameda, California

Norma Riccobuono
La Paloma High School
Brentwood, California

Mary Rose-Colley, DEd, CHES
Lock Haven University
Lock Haven, Pennsylvania

Judith K. Scheer, MEd, EdS, CHES
Contra Costa County Office of Education
Walnut Creek, California

Michael A. Smith, MS, CHES
Long Beach Unified School District
Long Beach, California

Janet L. Sola, PhD
YWCA of the U.S.A.
New York, New York

Susan K. Telljohnn, HSD
University of Toledo
Toledo, Ohio

Donna J. Underwood, MS
Consulting Public Health Administrator
Champaign, Illinois

Peggy Woosley
Stuttgart Public Schools
Stuttgart, Arkansas

Dale Zevin, MA
Educational Consultant
Watsonville, California

PROGRAM OVERVIEW

COMPONENTS

PROGRAM GOAL

Students will acquire the necessary skills and information to make healthy choices.

Choosing Health High School consists of 8 Teacher/Student Resource books in critical topics appropriate for the high school health curriculum. *Think, Choose, Act Healthy, High School* provides creative activities to augment the basic program. There are also 13 *Health Facts* books that provide additional content information for teachers.

- **Teacher/Student Resource Books**—These 8 books address key health topics, content and issues for high school students. All teacher/student information, instructional process, assessment tools and student activity masters for the particular topic are included in each book.
- ***Think, Choose, Act Healthy, High School***—This book provides 150 reproducible student activities that work hand in hand with the teacher/student resource books. They will challenge students to think and make their own personal health choices.
- ***Health Facts* Books**—These reference books provide clear, concise background information to support the resource books.

Program Overview

Components

Health Facts Books Correlation	
Resource Books	***Health Facts* Books**
Abstinence	Abstinence Sexuality
Body Image and Eating Disorders	Nutrition and Body Image
Communication and Self-Esteem	Self-Esteem and Mental Health
Fitness and Health	Fitness
STD and HIV	STD HIV Disease
Sexuality and Relationships	Sexuality
Tobacco, Alcohol and Drugs	Drugs Tobacco
Violence and Injury	Violence Injury Prevention

PROGRAM OVERVIEW

TEACHING STRATEGIES

Each resource book is designed so you can easily find the instructional content, process and skills. You can spend more time on teaching and less on planning. Special tools are provided to help you challenge your students, reach out to their families and assess student success.

A wide variety of learning opportunities is provided in each book to increase interest and meet the needs of different kinds of learners. Many are interactive, encouraging students to help each other learn. The **31** teaching strategies can be divided into 4 categories based on educational purpose. They are Informational, Creative Expression, Sharing Ideas and Opinions and Developing Critical Thinking. Descriptions of the teaching strategies are found in the appendix.

Providing Key Information

Students need information before they can move to higher-level thinking. This program uses a variety of strategies to provide the information students need to take actions for health. Strategies include:

- anonymous question box
- current events
- demonstrations
- experiments
- games and puzzles
- guest speakers
- information gathering
- interviewing
- oral presentations

Encouraging Creative Expression

Creative expression provides the opportunity to integrate language arts, fine arts and personal experience into learning. It also allows students the opportunity to demonstrate their understanding in ways that are unique to them. Creative expression encourages students to capitalize on their strengths and their interests. Strategies include:

- artistic expression
- creative writing
- dramatic presentations
- roleplays

Program Overview

Teaching Strategies

Sharing Ideas, Feelings and Opinions

In the sensitive area of health education, providing a safe atmosphere in which to discuss a variety of opinions and feelings is essential. Discussion provides the opportunity to clarify misinformation and correct misconceptions. Strategies include:

- brainstorming
- class discussion
- clustering
- continuum voting
- dyad discussion
- family discussion
- forced field analysis
- journal writing
- panel discussion
- self-assessment
- small groups
- surveys and inventories

Developing Critical Thinking

Critical thinking skills are crucial if students are to adopt healthy behaviors. Healthy choices necessitate the ability to become independent thinkers, analyze problems and devise solutions in real-life situations. Strategies include:

- case studies
- cooperative learning groups
- debates
- factual writing
- media analysis
- personal contracts
- research

PROGRAM OVERVIEW

SKILLS INFUSION

Studies of high-risk children and adolescents show that certain characteristics are common to children who succeed in adverse situations. These children are called resilient. Evaluation of educational programs designed to build resiliency has shown that several elements are important for success. The most important is the inclusion of activities designed to build personal and social skills.

Throughout each resource book, students practice skills along with the content addressed in the activities. Activities that naturally infuse personal and social skills are identified.

- **Communication**—Students with effective communication skills are able to express thoughts and feelings, actively listen to others, and give clear verbal and nonverbal messages related to health or any other aspect of their lives.
- **Decision Making**—Students with effective decision-making skills are able to identify decision points, gather information, and analyze and evaluate alternatives before they take action. This skill is important to promote positive health choices.
- **Assertiveness**—Students with effective assertiveness skills are able to resist pressure and influence from peers, advertising or others that may be in conflict with healthy behavior. This skill involves the ability to negotiate in stressful situations and refuse unwanted influences.
- **Stress Management**—Students with effective stress-management skills are able to cope with stress as a normal part of life. They are able to identify situations and conditions that produce stress and adopt healthy coping behaviors.
- **Goal Setting**—Students with effective goal-setting skills are able to clarify goals based on their needs and interests. They are able to set realistic goals, identify the sub-steps to goals, take action and evaluate their progress. They are able to learn from mistakes and change goals as needed.

Program Overview

Working with Families and Communities

A few general principles can help you be most effective in teaching about health:

- Establish a rapport with your students, their families and your community.
- Prepare yourself so that you are comfortable with the content and instructional process required to teach about fitness and health successfully.
- Be aware of state laws and guidelines established by your school district that relate to health.
- Invite parents and other family members to attend a preview of the materials.

Family involvement improves student learning. Encourage family members and other volunteers to help you in the classroom as you teach these activities.

WHY TEACH ABOUT ABSTINENCE?

Abstinence is the choice to refrain from sexual intercourse and is recognized and encouraged as the safest choice for teens. Many teens do want to be abstinent, yet the many influences surrounding them—peers, media, advertising—cause pressure to become sexually active. Teens need the opportunity to consider the benefits of abstinence in their own lives and receive the education necessary to make this choice work for them.

Teens need to be given the opportunity to understand that sexuality is a part of their total being and that abstinence is a good choice. Training in using the skills for decision making, communication, refusing and assertiveness as they consider their choices of sexual behavior encourages safer behavior. Teens are aware of the risks of being sexually active, including pregnancy, STD and HIV; yet they usually don't believe these things can happen to them. Understanding the risks and the consequences in a personal way can encourage teens to choose abstinence. Abstinence is greatly needed to help teens choose to be safe.

Abstinence and High School Students

At no time is the pressure to be sexually active greater for adolescents than in high school. The combination of increased freedom of time and the emerging sense of self-determination (as well as rejection of parental control) leaves teens vulnerable to sexual activity that can be physically and emotionally harmful. Many teens today lack the positive role models that can lead them to make good choices. Some have low self-esteem and tend to make choices that are harmful. The media surrounds them with tantalizing messages encouraging sexual activity. Their own peers often pressure them in ways that encourage sexual involvement. Because the opportunity to become sexually active is so great, this is a difficult time for teens to remain abstinent.

Abstinence education can be viewed on a variety of levels. Abstinence is the only sure way to prevent the spread of many sexually transmitted diseases. One in 8 teens contract a sexually transmitted disease annually. Some of these diseases are not curable; and some can be fatal. HIV infection is spreading rapidly among teens today. Thus, disease prevention is an important reason for abstinence education.

Pregnancy prevention is another rationale for abstinence education. There are more than 1 million teen pregnancies each year—80% are unplanned. The resulting abortions or births and possible parenthood are life-changing events that most teens are not ready to face. Preventing unplanned pregnancies in teens is an excellent reason for abstinence education.

The Abstinence Resource Book

Why Teach About Abstinence?

The development of relationships is part of teens' growth and development. The plunge into sexual activity often happens too much too soon and causes much emotional turmoil. The gradual development of a maturing relationship—one that can lead to love, which can later be expressed by sexual involvement—can be enriching and rewarding. Most high school teens are not mature enough to experience this development. Abstinence can allow teens time to mature until they are able to enjoy such a relationship.

A further reason for abstinence education for teens that is shared by many is the moral/religious perspective. Many adults and teens share the belief that premarital sexual involvement is to be avoided. Abstinence education can provide teens with the skills needed to follow through on moral or religious convictions.

Family Activities

By encouraging parents' role as sexuality educators of their children, schools join forces with the home to provide support and guidance for teens in this often confusing area. The purpose of Family Activities is to increase family communication about sexuality. The confidential activities for families in this resource book provide an opportunity for parents to share their values with their teens. Activities encourage exchange of views and sharing of information, using clear communication and active listening.

Parents can be informed of the family activities by a letter sent home at the beginning of the units. Activity sheets can be provided as a packet before beginning the units or sent home one at a time.

Background Information About Abstinence

Instant Expert sections throughout this book give you all the information you need to teach each unit.

The Abstinence Resource Book

Objectives

Students Will Be Able to:

Unit 1: Sexuality and Myths

1. Define sexuality.
2. Identify myths about sexual behavior.

Unit 2: A World of Pressure

1. Identify both internal and external pressures to be sexually active.
2. Identify media sources of sexual pressure and their effects on teens.
3. Identify influences for sexual responsibility, or abstinence.

Unit 3: Risks and Decisions

1. Describe the influence of risk-taking behavior on sexual decision making.
2. Apply the decision-making process and STAR method to examples of situations of sexual temptation.

Unit 4: No in Words and Actions

1. Demonstrate the use of listening skills and I-statements.
2. Demonstrate the use of assertive communication.
3. Demonstrate the use of delay and refusal skills.

SAMPLE LETTER AND PERMISSION SLIP

Dear Family,

Your son or daughter will be involved in a series of lessons on sexual abstinence. Because we believe that parents are the primary sexuality educators of their children, we are encouraging students to discuss what they learn in class with their families.

To reinforce the partnership between home and school, several Family Activity opportunities are included throughout the lessons on sexuality and abstinence. These activities offer a way for parents to be involved in the classroom learning and to reinforce their family's moral, religious and ethical beliefs.

Family activity sheets will be sent home with students throughout the course. These activities can be previewed by contacting me at school.

Please know that:

- Use of the activities is voluntary.
- Credit will be given but there will be alternate assignments for students whose parents choose not to participate.
- Receipt of the activities does not obligate you to use them.
- The activities are confidential and will not be returned to school. They are for the private benefit of students and their families.
- You will be asked to complete and sign a short feedback form that your son or daughter will return to class as evidence of completing the assignment.

I hope that you will find these materials valuable. We will appreciate any comments you may have about them.

Sincerely,

____

- -

Please complete and return to school.

☐ I would like to have the activities sent home with my student as they are assigned.

☐ Please send the packet of activities home for me to preview. I will complete them as I choose, as they are assigned.

Name ______________________________

Phone ______________________________

Address ______________________________

Anatomy of a Unit

Preparing to Teach

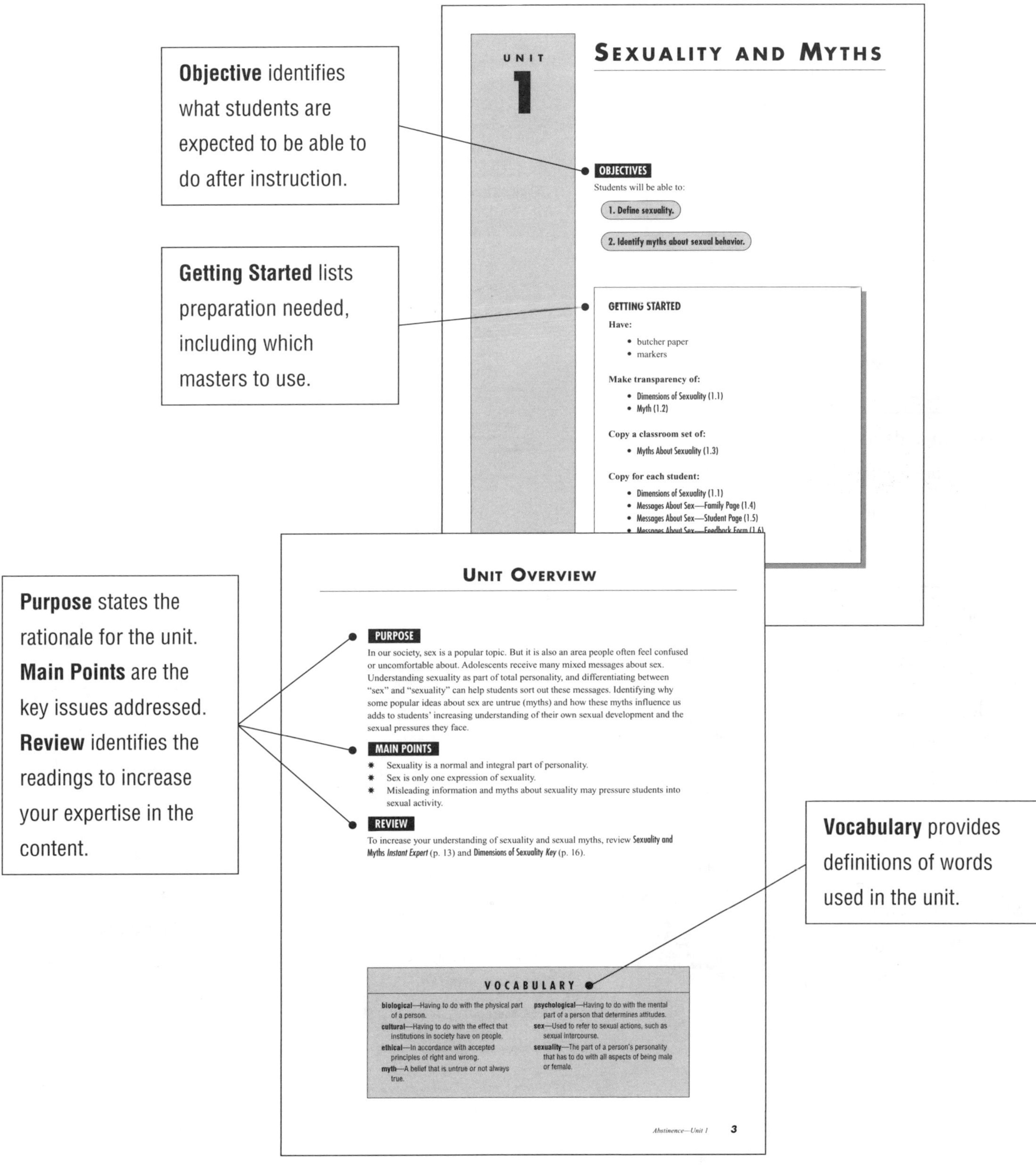

Anatomy of a Unit

Teaching the Activities

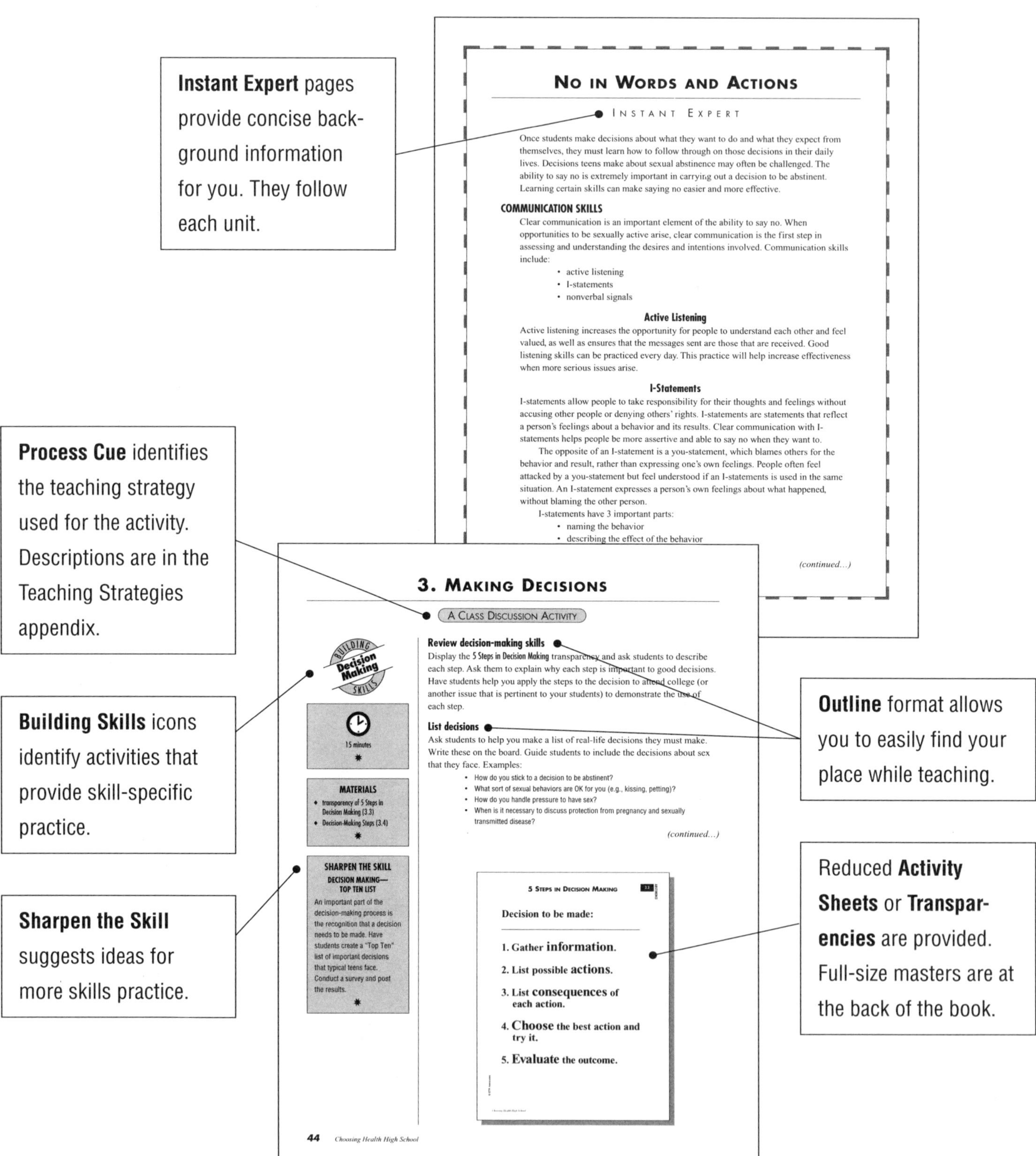

No in Words and Actions

Instant Expert

Once students make decisions about what they want to do and what they expect from themselves, they must learn how to follow through on those decisions in their daily lives. Decisions teens make about sexual abstinence may often be challenged. The ability to say no is extremely important in carrying out a decision to be abstinent. Learning certain skills can make saying no easier and more effective.

COMMUNICATION SKILLS

Clear communication is an important element of the ability to say no. When opportunities to be sexually active arise, clear communication is the first step in assessing and understanding the desires and intentions involved. Communication skills include:

- active listening
- I-statements
- nonverbal signals

Active Listening

Active listening increases the opportunity for people to understand each other and feel valued, as well as ensures that the messages sent are those that are received. Good listening skills can be practiced every day. This practice will help increase effectiveness when more serious issues arise.

I-Statements

I-statements allow people to take responsibility for their thoughts and feelings without accusing other people or denying others' rights. I-statements are statements that reflect a person's feelings about a behavior and its results. Clear communication with I-statements helps people be more assertive and able to say no when they want to.

The opposite of an I-statement is a you-statement, which blames others for the behavior and result, rather than expressing one's own feelings. People often feel attacked by a you-statement but feel understood if an I-statement is used in the same situation. An I-statement expresses a person's own feelings about what happened, without blaming the other person.

I-statements have 3 important parts:

- naming the behavior
- describing the effect of the behavior

(continued...)

3. Making Decisions

A Class Discussion Activity

Review decision-making skills
Display the **5 Steps in Decision Making** transparency and ask students to describe each step. Ask them to explain why each step is important to good decisions. Have students help you apply the steps to the decision to attend college (or another issue that is pertinent to your students) to demonstrate the use of each step.

List decisions
Ask students to help you make a list of real-life decisions they must make. Write these on the board. Guide students to include the decisions about sex that they face. Examples:

- How do you stick to a decision to be abstinent?
- What sort of sexual behaviors are OK for you (e.g., kissing, petting)?
- How do you handle pressure to have sex?
- When is it necessary to discuss protection from pregnancy and sexually transmitted disease?

(continued...)

MATERIALS

- transparency of 5 Steps in Decision Making (3.3)
- Decision-Making Steps (3.4)

SHARPEN THE SKILL

DECISION MAKING—TOP TEN LIST

An important part of the decision-making process is the recognition that a decision needs to be made. Have students create a "Top Ten" list of important decisions that typical teens face. Conduct a survey and post the results.

5 Steps in Decision Making

Decision to be made:

1. Gather information.
2. List possible actions.
3. List consequences of each action.
4. Choose the best action and try it.
5. Evaluate the outcome.

44 *Choosing Health High School*

Anatomy of a Unit

Special Features

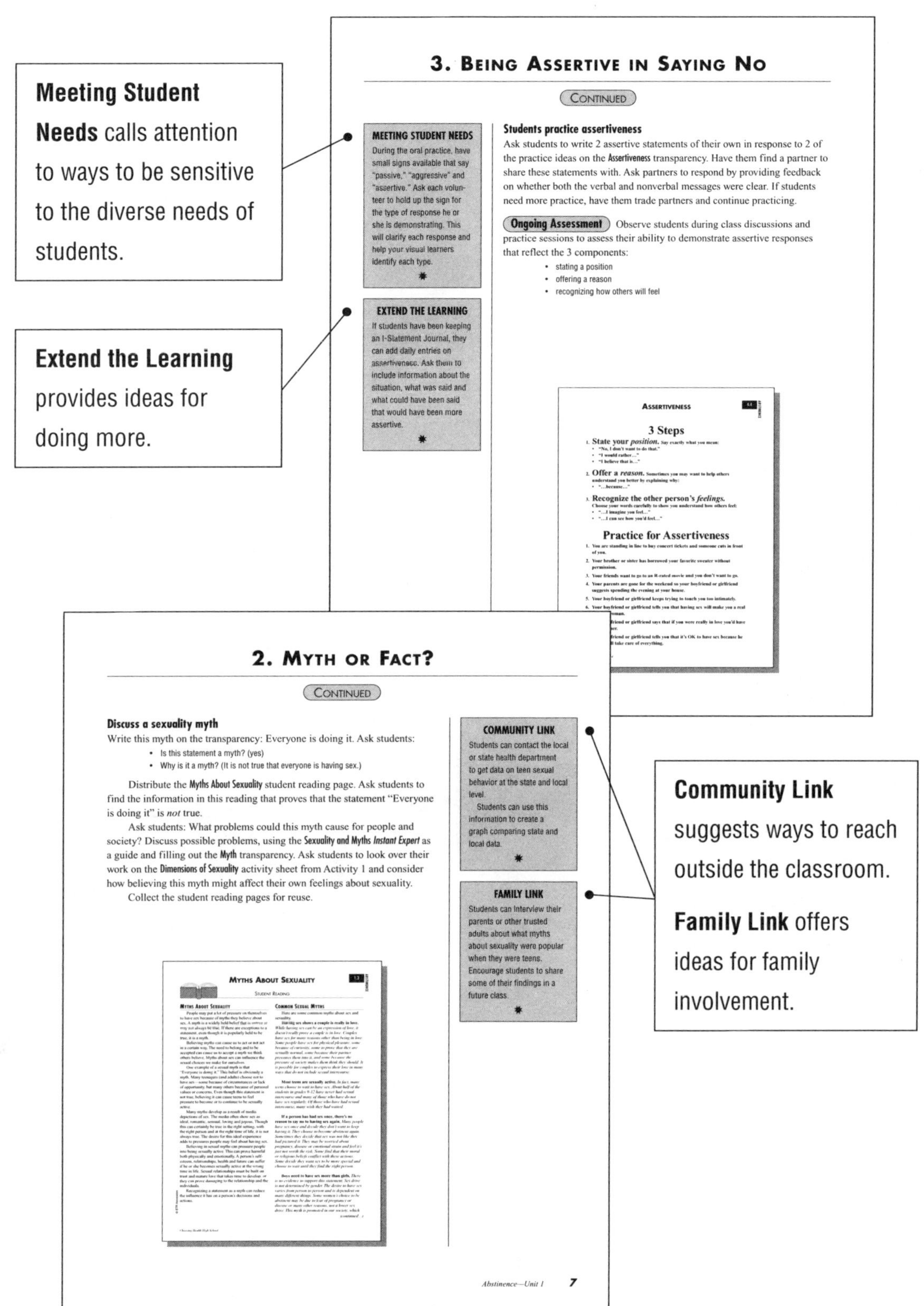

Meeting Student Needs calls attention to ways to be sensitive to the diverse needs of students.

Extend the Learning provides ideas for doing more.

3. Being Assertive in Saying No

(Continued)

MEETING STUDENT NEEDS
During the oral practice, have small signs available that say "passive," "aggressive" and "assertive." Ask each volunteer to hold up the sign for the type of response he or she is demonstrating. This will clarify each response and help your visual learners identify each type.

EXTEND THE LEARNING
If students have been keeping an I-Statement Journal, they can add daily entries on assertiveness. Ask them to include information about the situation, what was said and what could have been said that would have been more assertive.

Students practice assertiveness
Ask students to write 2 assertive statements of their own in response to 2 of the practice ideas on the **Assertiveness** transparency. Have them find a partner to share these statements with. Ask partners to respond by providing feedback on whether both the verbal and nonverbal messages were clear. If students need more practice, have them trade partners and continue practicing.

Ongoing Assessment Observe students during class discussions and practice sessions to assess their ability to demonstrate assertive responses that reflect the 3 components:

- stating a position
- offering a reason
- recognizing how others will feel

Assertiveness

3 Steps

1. State your *position*.
2. Offer a *reason*.
3. Recognize the other person's *feelings*.

Practice for Assertiveness

2. Myth or Fact?

(Continued)

Discuss a sexuality myth
Write this myth on the transparency: Everyone is doing it. Ask students:

- Is this statement a myth? (yes)
- Why is it a myth? (It is not true that everyone is having sex.)

Distribute the **Myths About Sexuality** student reading page. Ask students to find the information in this reading that proves that the statement "Everyone is doing it" is *not* true.

Ask students: What problems could this myth cause for people and society? Discuss possible problems, using the **Sexuality and Myths *Instant Expert*** as a guide and filling out the **Myth** transparency. Ask students to look over their work on the **Dimensions of Sexuality** activity sheet from Activity 1 and consider how believing this myth might affect their own feelings about sexuality.

Collect the student reading pages for reuse.

Myths About Sexuality

Student Reading

COMMUNITY LINK
Students can contact the local or state health department to get data on teen sexual behavior at the state and local level.
Students can use this information to create a graph comparing state and local data.

FAMILY LINK
Students can interview their parents or other trusted adults about what myths about sexuality were popular when they were teens. Encourage students to share some of their findings in a future class.

Abstinence—Unit 1 7

Community Link suggests ways to reach outside the classroom.

Family Link offers ideas for family involvement.

ANATOMY OF A UNIT

EVALUATION FEATURES

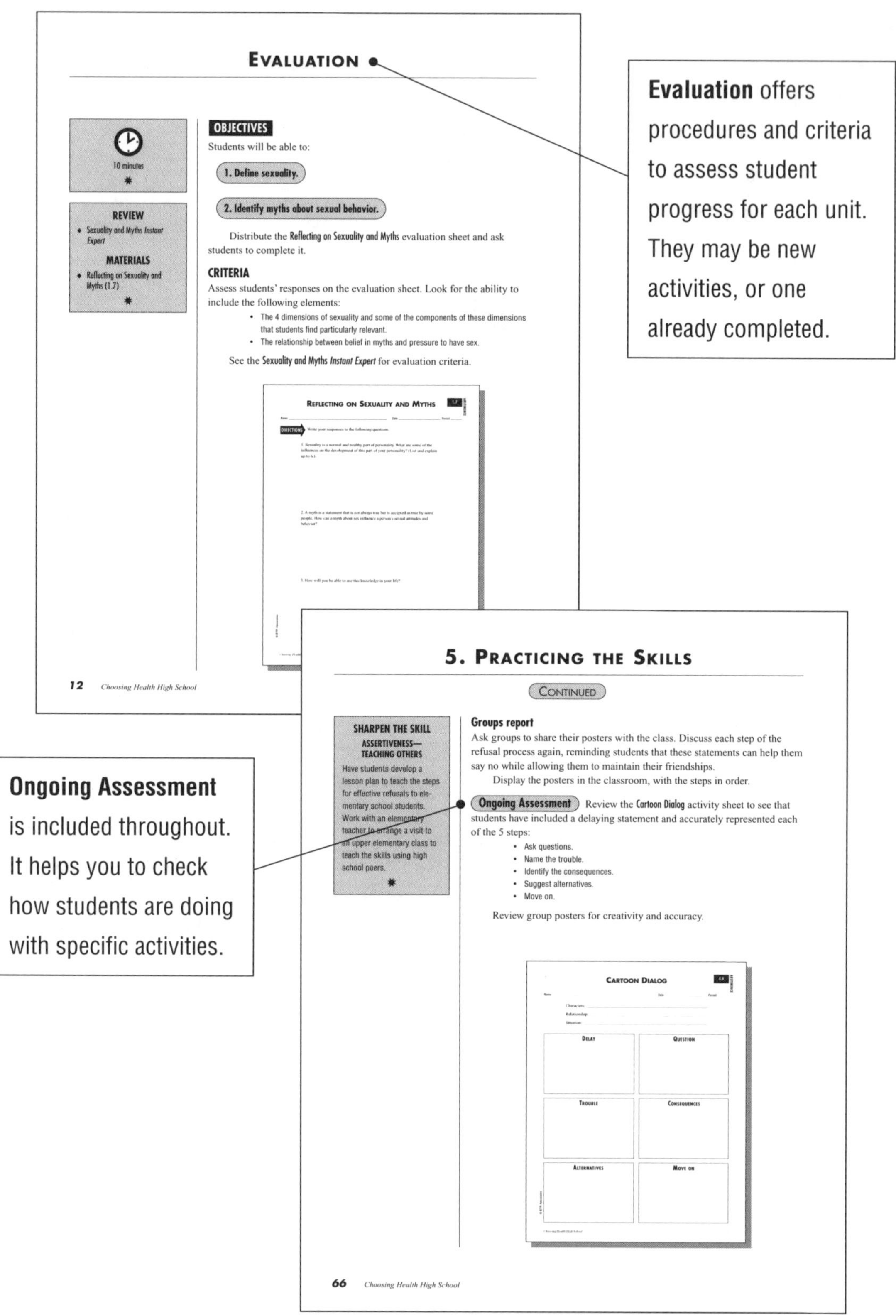

UNIT

1

SEXUALITY AND MYTHS

TIME

2–3 periods

ACTIVITIES

1. Sex or Sexuality?
2. Myth or Fact?
3. Sexuality Myths
4. Messages About Sex

UNIT

1

Sexuality and Myths

OBJECTIVES

Students will be able to:

1. Define sexuality.

2. Identify myths about sexual behavior.

GETTING STARTED

Have:

- butcher paper
- markers

Make transparency of:

- Dimensions of Sexuality (1.1)
- Myth (1.2)

Copy a classroom set of:

- Myths About Sexuality (1.3)

Copy for each student:

- Dimensions of Sexuality (1.1)
- Messages About Sex—Family Page (1.4)
- Messages About Sex—Student Page (1.5)
- Messages About Sex—Feedback Form (1.6)
- Reflecting on Sexuality and Myths (1.7)

UNIT OVERVIEW

PURPOSE

In our society, sex is a popular topic. But it is also an area people often feel confused or uncomfortable about. Adolescents receive many mixed messages about sex. Understanding sexuality as part of total personality, and differentiating between "sex" and "sexuality" can help students sort out these messages. Identifying why some popular ideas about sex are untrue (myths) and how these myths influence us adds to students' increasing understanding of their own sexual development and the sexual pressures they face.

MAIN POINTS

* Sexuality is a normal and integral part of personality.
* Sex is only one expression of sexuality.
* Misleading information and myths about sexuality may pressure students into sexual activity.

REVIEW

To increase your understanding of sexuality and sexual myths, review **Sexuality and Myths *Instant Expert*** (p. 13) and **Dimensions of Sexuality *Key*** (p. 16).

VOCABULARY

biological—Having to do with the physical part of a person.

cultural—Having to do with the effect that institutions in society have on people.

ethical—In accordance with accepted principles of right and wrong.

myth—A belief that is untrue or not always true.

psychological—Having to do with the mental part of a person that determines attitudes.

sex—Used to refer to sexual actions, such as sexual intercourse.

sexuality—The part of a person's personality that has to do with all aspects of being male or female.

1. Sex or Sexuality?

A Class Discussion and Self-Assessment Activity

30 minutes

MATERIALS

- transparency of Dimensions of Sexuality (1.1)
- Dimensions of Sexuality (1.1)

Define *sexuality*

Write the word *sexuality* on the board. Ask students: How would you define this word?

Write the word *sex* on the board. How would students define this word? Suggest definitions such as the following:

- **sex**—expressing sexual feelings in a sexual act such as intercourse
- **sexuality**—part of human personality; includes all aspects of being male or female

Write these definitions on the board.

Help students understand that a clear understanding of their own sexuality will help them cope with sexual pressures in their lives and make the decisions that are best for them.

Discuss sex and sexuality

Discuss the differences between sex and sexuality, using the **Sexuality and Myths *Instant Expert*** as a guide.

(continued...)

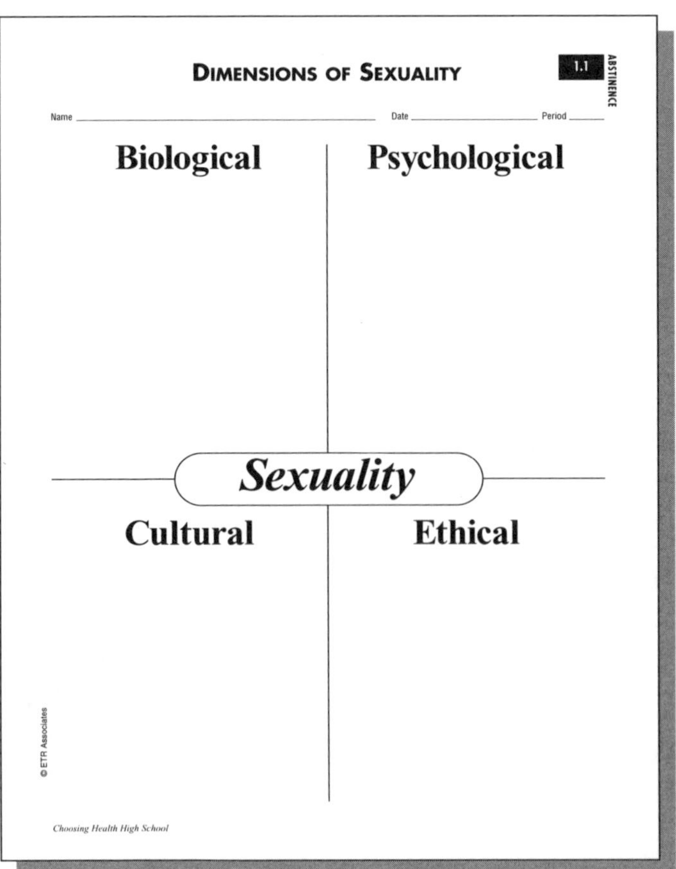

Dimensions of Sexuality

1.1 ABSTINENCE

Name ____________ Date ________ Period ______

Biological | Psychological

Sexuality

Cultural | Ethical

© ETR Associates

Choosing Health High School

1. Sex or Sexuality?

Continued

Discuss dimensions of sexuality

Distribute the **Dimensions of Sexuality** activity sheet and display the **Dimensions of Sexuality** transparency. Briefly describe each of the 4 dimensions of sexuality—biological, psychological, cultural and ethical—using the **Sexuality and Myths** ***Instant Expert*** as a guide. Point out that all of these aspects of sexuality influence people's personality.

Ask students for examples of each dimension. Write responses on the transparency. See the **Dimensions of Sexuality** ***Key.***

Ask students to write 3 or more examples of each dimension on the activity sheet. They can choose the examples that make the most sense to them.

Students analyze influences

Have students turn the activity sheet over and write a response to the following question. Emphasize that their answers will be private.

- What are the strongest influences from each dimension of sexuality in your life?

Discuss influences in general after the writing assignment. Do not ask students to disclose personal information about the influences they listed.

MEETING STUDENT NEEDS

To accomplish the goals of these lessons, students need to feel comfortable talking about sexuality and sexual pressure. Establishing groundrules for classroom discussions helps establish an atmosphere of trust and comfort.

2. Myth or Fact?

A Class Discussion Activity

15 minutes

MATERIALS

- transparency of Myth (1.2)
- classroom set of Myths About Sexuality (1.3)
- completed Dimensions of Sexuality (1.1), from Activity 1

✷

Discuss myths

Display the **Myth** transparency. Ask students what a myth is. After a few responses, write a definition on the transparency. Possible definition:

- A belief that is untrue or may not always be true.

Discuss myths, using the **Sexuality and Myths *Instant Expert*** as a guide. Ask students:

- How do myths develop?
- Can myths cause problems for people or society?
- Do you see a relationship between myths and the psychological, cultural or ethical dimensions of sexuality?

(continued...)

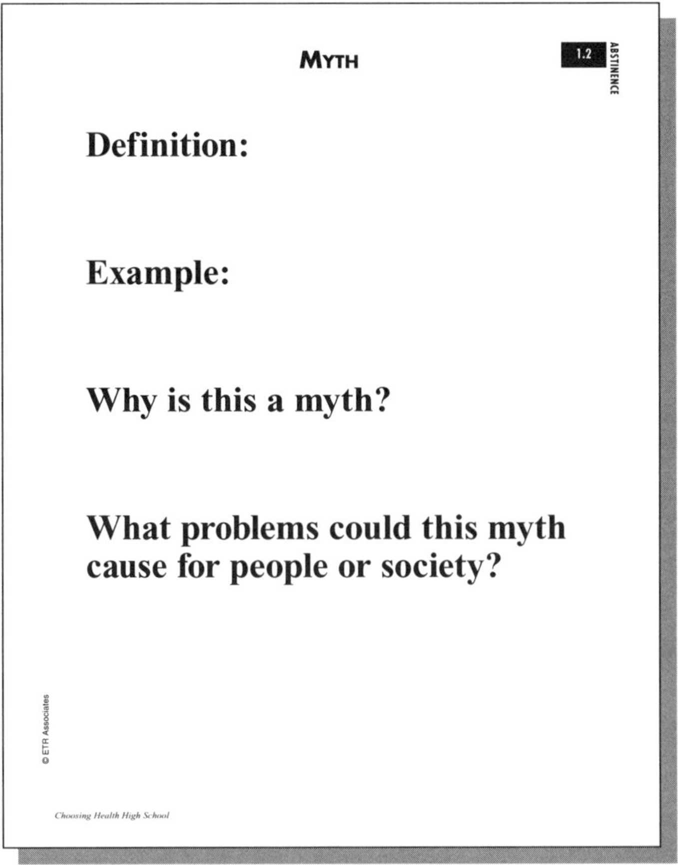
MYTH

1.2 ABSTINENCE

Definition:

Example:

Why is this a myth?

What problems could this myth cause for people or society?

© ETR Associates

Choosing Health High School

2. Myth or Fact?

Continued

Discuss a sexuality myth

Write this myth on the transparency: Everyone is doing it. Ask students:

- Is this statement a myth? (yes)
- Why is it a myth? (It is not true that everyone is having sex.)

Distribute the **Myths About Sexuality** student reading page. Ask students to find the information in this reading that proves that the statement "Everyone is doing it" is *not* true.

Ask students: What problems could this myth cause for people and society? Discuss possible problems, using the **Sexuality and Myths *Instant Expert*** as a guide and filling out the **Myth** transparency. Ask students to look over their work on the **Dimensions of Sexuality** activity sheet from Activity 1 and consider how believing this myth might affect their own feelings about sexuality.

Collect the student reading pages for reuse.

Myths About Sexuality

1.3 ABSTINENCE

Student Reading

Myths About Sexuality

People may put a lot of pressure on themselves to have sex because of myths they believe about sex. A myth is a widely held belief that is untrue or may not always be true. If there are exceptions to a statement, even though it is popularly held to be true, it is a myth.

Believing myths can cause us to act or not act in a certain way. The need to belong and to be accepted can cause us to accept a myth we think others believe. Myths about sex can influence the sexual choices we make for ourselves.

One example of a sexual myth is that "Everyone is doing it." This belief is obviously a myth. Many teenagers (and adults) choose not to have sex—some because of circumstances or lack of opportunity, but many others because of personal values or concerns. Even though this statement is not true, believing it can cause teens to feel pressure to become or to continue to be sexually active.

Many myths develop as a result of media depictions of sex. The media often show sex as ideal, romantic, sensual, loving and joyous. Though this can certainly be true in the right setting, with the right person and at the right time of life, it is not always true. The desire for this ideal experience adds to pressures people may feel about having sex.

Believing in sexual myths can pressure people into being sexually active. This can prove harmful both physically and emotionally. A person's self-esteem, relationships, health and future can suffer if he or she becomes sexually active at the wrong time in life. Sexual relationships must be built on trust and mature love that takes time to develop, or they can prove damaging to the relationship and the individuals.

Recognizing a statement as a myth can reduce the influence it has on a person's decisions and actions.

Common Sexual Myths

Here are some common myths about sex and sexuality.

Having sex shows a couple is really in love. *While having sex can be an expression of love, it doesn't really prove a couple is in love. Couples have sex for many reasons other than being in love. Some people have sex for physical pleasure, some because of curiosity, some to prove that they are sexually normal, some because their partner pressures them into it, and some because the pressure of society makes them think they should. It is possible for couples to express their love in many ways that do not include sexual intercourse.*

Most teens are sexually active. *In fact, many teens choose to wait to have sex. About half of the students in grades 9-12 have never had sexual intercourse and many of those who have do not have sex regularly. Of those who have had sexual intercourse, many wish they had waited.*

If a person has had sex once, there's no reason to say no to having sex again. *Many people have sex once and decide they don't want to keep having it. They choose to become abstinent again. Sometimes they decide that sex was not like they had pictured it. They may be worried about pregnancy, disease or emotional strain and feel it's just not worth the risk. Some find that their moral or religious beliefs conflict with these actions. Some decide they want sex to be more special and choose to wait until they find the right person.*

Boys need to have sex more than girls. *There is no evidence to support this statement. Sex drive is not determined by gender. The desire to have sex varies from person to person and is dependent on many different things. Some women's choice to be abstinent may be due to fear of pregnancy or disease or many other reasons, not a lower sex drive. This myth is promoted in our society, which*

(continued...)

Choosing Health High School

EXTEND THE LEARNING

Students can contact the local or state health department to get data on teen sexual behavior at the state and local level.

Students can use this information to create a graph comparing state and local data.

FAMILY LINK

Students can interview their parents or other trusted adults about what myths about sexuality were popular when they were teens. Encourage students to share some of their findings in a future class.

3. Sexuality Myths

A Brainstorming and Small Group Activity

45 minutes

MATERIALS

- butcher paper
- markers
- classroom set of Myths About Sexuality (1.3)

✷

MEETING STUDENT NEEDS

Groups of 4–6 usually work well for the activity. If students seem shy or too uncomfortable, use smaller groups. Remind students of class groundrules and stress that laughter is OK. If laughter or other signs of nervousness occur, acknowledge that it can be embarrassing to talk about these issues. Encourage students to participate despite their embarrassment and stress the importance of being able to discuss sexuality issues in a straightforward, honest way.

Brainstorm myths

Conduct a brainstorming session to identify myths about sex and sexuality that students have heard. Write responses on the board. Use information from the **Sexuality and Myths *Instant Expert*** to add to the list. Be sure to list enough myths to have 1 for each group of 4–6 students.

Groups evaluate myths

Divide class into groups of 4–6. Distribute the **Myths About Sexuality** student reading page. Give each group a piece of butcher paper and a marker, and assign a different myth to each group. Explain the group assignment:

- Choose a recorder, a reporter and a timekeeper.
- The recorder should divide the paper into 3 columns and write "Myth" at the top of the first column, "Proof" at the top of the second and "Problems" at the top of the third.
- Then the recorder should write the myth assigned to your group in the column titled "Myth."
- Discuss why the statement is a myth.
- Use the **Myths About Sexuality** student reading page to find information that proves the statement is a myth. The recorder should write this information in the column titled "Proof."
- Discuss the problems that could arise if teens believe this myth. Write these problems in the column titled "Problems."
- Prepare a report for the class.

(continued...)

3. Sexuality Myths

Continued

Groups report

Have group reporters post the butcher paper sheets in the classroom and share the group conclusions. Discuss the findings. Be ready to add information or correct misconceptions as needed. You may want to keep group work posted for a few days.

Collect the student reading pages for reuse.

Ongoing Assessment Observe the accuracy and depth of the information provided by the groups. See the **Sexuality and Myths *Instant Expert*** for specific criteria.

FAMILY LINK

Ask students to identify any of the myths listed by the class that adults they talked to also noted. What myths that are no longer popular did they hear from the adults?

4. Messages About Sex

A Family Discussion Activity

5 minutes, plus follow-up

MATERIALS

- Messages About Sex—Family Page (1.4)
- Messages About Sex—Student Page (1.5)
- Messages About Sex—Feedback Form (1.6)

✷

MEETING STUDENT NEEDS

Students may need some encouragement to try the family activity, but will probably find that it can be a rewarding experience. In class you might ask half of the students to act as parents and list reasons it is sometimes hard for them to talk about sex with their teens. Ask the other half to make a list of why teens find it difficult to talk to their parents. Compare the 2 lists and discuss the similarities. Use this as an introduction to develop some guidelines for family activity use throughout the units.

Initiate family activity

Explain that parents and family are a primary influence on values about sexuality, so it makes sense to involve them in s held in class.

Distribute the **Messages About Sex—Family Page, Student Page** a . Ask students to take the activity sheets home and complete t with their parents or other adult family members.

Assure students that specific experiences will not be shared in class. This activity is an opportunity for them to have a confidential discussion with their parent(s).

(continued...)

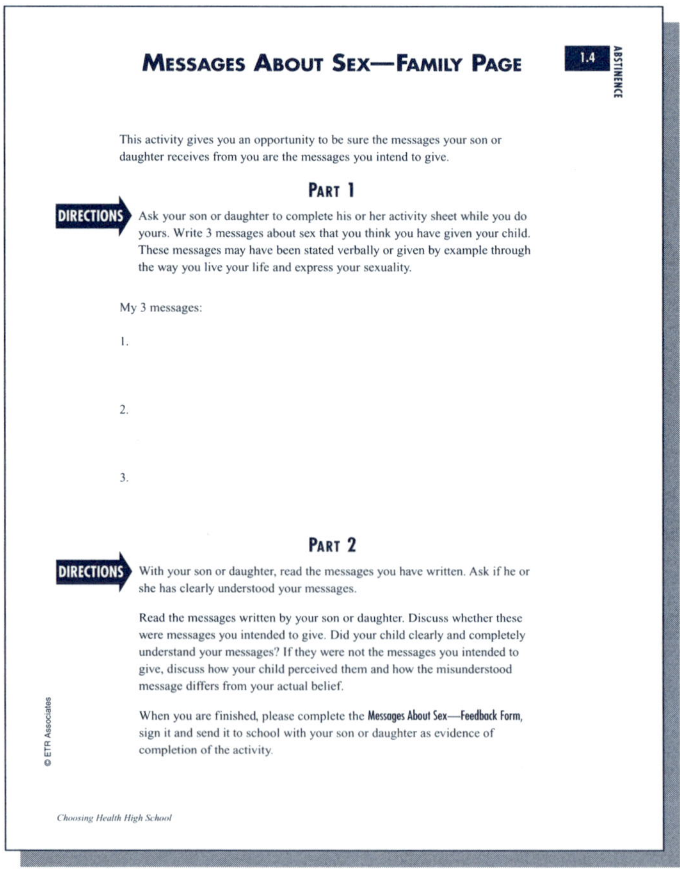

Messages About Sex—Family Page 1.4 ABSTINENCE

This activity gives you an opportunity to be sure the messages your son or daughter receives from you are the messages you intend to give.

Part 1

DIRECTIONS Ask your son or daughter to complete his or her activity sheet while you do yours. Write 3 messages about sex that you think you have given your child. These messages may have been stated verbally or given by example through the way you live your life and express your sexuality.

My 3 messages:

1.

2.

3.

Part 2

DIRECTIONS With your son or daughter, read the messages you have written. Ask if he or she has clearly understood your messages.

Read the messages written by your son or daughter. Discuss whether these were messages you intended to give. Did your child clearly and completely understand your messages? If they were not the messages you intended to give, discuss how your child perceived them and how the misunderstood message differs from your actual belief.

When you are finished, please complete the **Messages About Sex—Feedback Form**, sign it and send it to school with your son or daughter as evidence of completion of the activity.

© ETR Associates

Choosing Health High School

4. Messages About Sex

Continued

Discuss family activity

Explain that communication with families about sexuality issues may be difficult, but is essential because families can help students define their values about sexuality. Have students discuss the family activity in general terms. Ask students:

- Were you surprised by anything your parent(s) said?
- Was your parent surprised by anything you said?
- Did this activity help you become more clear on what you and/or your family believe?
- Do you think activities like these are useful? Why or why not?

Collect the **Feedback Forms** to give students credit for completing the assignment.

MEETING STUDENT NEEDS

Some parents may elect not to participate in the family activities. Be sure to provide an alternate way of earning credit for students whose family life may make completion of the assignment difficult. Students could complete the activity with an adult friend or mentor, or could complete only the student part of the assignment along with the **Feedback Form.**

Ensure privacy by collecting only the **Feedback Forms,** not the activity sheets.

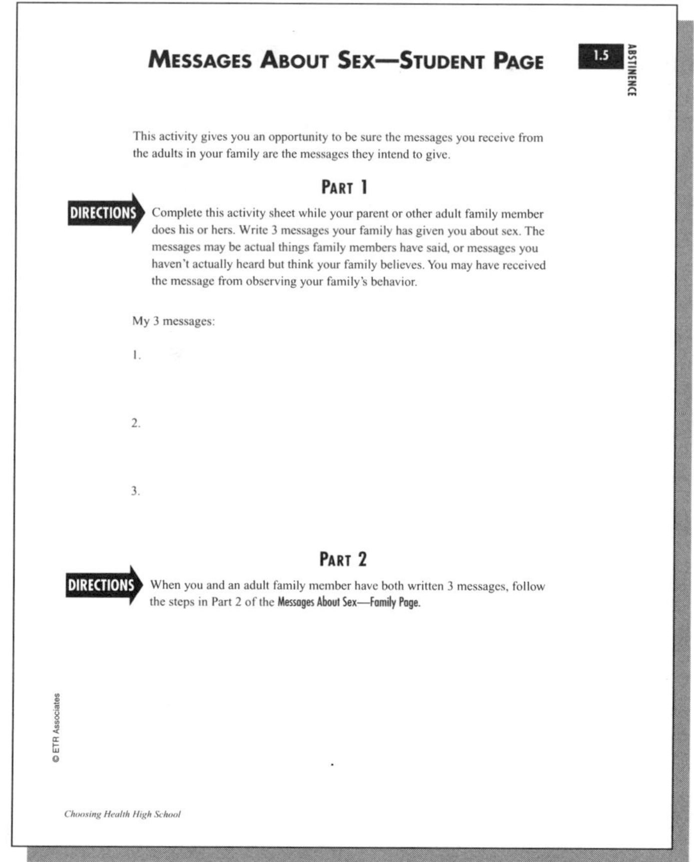

MESSAGES ABOUT SEX—STUDENT PAGE 1.5 ABSTINENCE

This activity gives you an opportunity to be sure the messages you receive from the adults in your family are the messages they intend to give.

PART 1

DIRECTIONS Complete this activity sheet while your parent or other adult family member does his or hers. Write 3 messages your family has given you about sex. The messages may be actual things family members have said, or messages you haven't actually heard but think your family believes. You may have received the message from observing your family's behavior.

My 3 messages:

1.

2.

3.

PART 2

DIRECTIONS When you and an adult family member have both written 3 messages, follow the steps in Part 2 of the **Messages About Sex—Family Page.**

Choosing Health High School

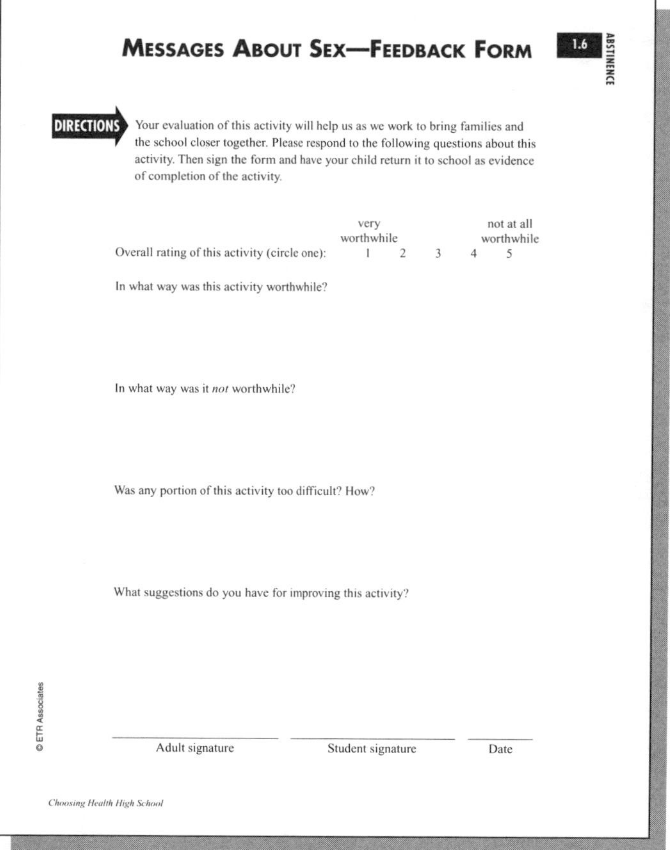

MESSAGES ABOUT SEX—FEEDBACK FORM 1.6 ABSTINENCE

DIRECTIONS Your evaluation of this activity will help us as we work to bring families and the school closer together. Please respond to the following questions about this activity. Then sign the form and have your child return it to school as evidence of completion of the activity.

Overall rating of this activity (circle one): very worthwhile 1 2 3 4 5 not at all worthwhile

In what way was this activity worthwhile?

In what way was it *not* worthwhile?

Was any portion of this activity too difficult? How?

What suggestions do you have for improving this activity?

Adult signature Student signature Date

Choosing Health High School

Evaluation

10 minutes

REVIEW

- Sexuality and Myths *Instant Expert*

MATERIALS

- Reflecting on Sexuality and Myths (1.7)

✸

OBJECTIVES

Students will be able to:

1. Define sexuality.

2. Identify myths about sexual behavior.

Distribute the **Reflecting on Sexuality and Myths** evaluation sheet and ask students to complete it.

CRITERIA

Assess students' responses on the evaluation sheet. Look for the ability to include the following elements:

- The 4 dimensions of sexuality and some of the components of these dimensions that students find particularly relevant.
- The relationship between belief in myths and pressure to have sex.

See the **Sexuality and Myths *Instant Expert*** for evaluation criteria.

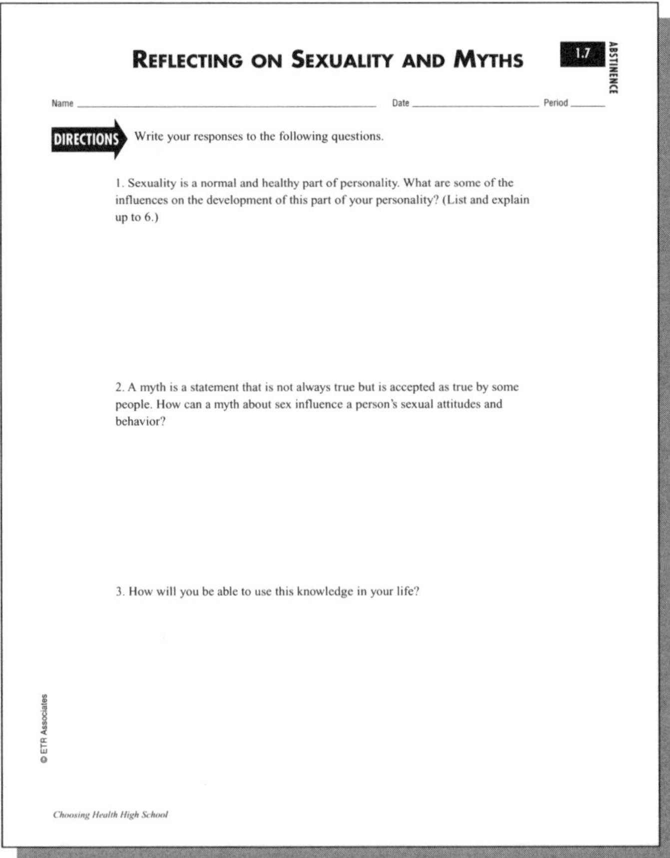

Reflecting on Sexuality and Myths 1.7 ABSTINENCE

Name ______ Date ______ Period ______

DIRECTIONS Write your responses to the following questions.

1. Sexuality is a normal and healthy part of personality. What are some of the influences on the development of this part of your personality? (List and explain up to 6.)

2. A myth is a statement that is not always true but is accepted as true by some people. How can a myth about sex influence a person's sexual attitudes and behavior?

3. How will you be able to use this knowledge in your life?

© ETR Associates

Choosing Health High School

SEXUALITY AND MYTHS

INSTANT EXPERT

Being sexual is a natural and normal part of life. Acting sexually, choosing to be sexually active, is an important decision that can influence the future of a person's life. To understand more about ourselves and our interest in sex, we must recognize that sexuality is part of our personality. As we grow, we develop our sexuality, just as we develop physically, emotionally and socially.

In the United States, sex is a very popular topic. Sexual behavior is portrayed on television and in films. Advertising often uses sexual imaging to sell products. Yet, despite our society's focus on sex, many people have anxieties or are confused about it.

Teens hear and believe many myths about sex. They are at a time of life when sexual concerns and questions are many. The ability to recognize a myth and an understanding of how myths can influence attitudes and behavior will help teens cope with the sexual pressures they may face. Teens also need to learn that there is a difference between "sex" and "sexuality."

WHAT IS SEXUALITY?

The term *sex* is usually used to refer to only 1 aspect of sexuality: actions. Sex usually refers to sexual intercourse or other very intimate sexual acts. *Sexuality* is a part of all of us from the time we are born, whether we express our sexuality through actions or not. Discussing sexuality in a broader sense, as more than sex, helps to clarify that sexuality is a part of every person's total personality.

The term *sexuality* refers to the part of our personality that has to do with being male or female, masculine and feminine. Sexuality has several dimensions. These dimensions are interconnected and each influences how we see ourselves at different stages of life. Sexuality does not suddenly emerge at puberty. It is part of personality development from birth. The important dimensions of sexuality include:

- biological
- psychological
- cultural
- ethical

Biological: The biological dimension of sexuality is often thought of as the only part because it is the most obvious. It is very important to recognize that the biological functions of sexuality are a natural part of being human. Biological aspects of sexuality include physical appearance, growth and development, sexual characteristics, sexual desire and response, and the physical ability to reproduce. Although humans cannot reproduce until puberty, our biological sexuality (erotic function) begins at birth.

(continued...)

Sexuality and Myths

Instant Expert

Psychological: The psychological dimension of sexuality consists of our attitudes and feelings about ourselves as sexual beings. These attitudes and feelings develop continually, beginning very early in life. We have models for and are given direction as to how to think and act as we experience our sexual development. Emotions, life experiences, attitudes about ourselves and others, expressiveness and motivation to act, along with learned behaviors, influence the psychological part of our sexuality.

Cultural: Culture also plays a big role in how our sexuality develops as part of personality. Current as well as historical culture affects our thoughts and actions. Gender roles, sexual customs and laws, and the models we see in society make up this cultural environment. Influences on the cultural dimension of sexuality include the family, neighbors, peers, religious expression, school, dating habits, advertising and the media.

Ethical: Ethics, the concept of right and wrong, also affects our sexuality. Our family's values, religious beliefs, personal values and accepted morals influence this dimension.

Teens need to understand that all of these areas influence how we see and accept ourselves as sexual beings. The more they understand their own sexuality, the more they will be able to be comfortable with sexual issues and make good decisions about the expression of their sexuality.

THE ROLE OF MYTH

People may put a lot of pressure on themselves to have sex because of myths they believe about sex. A myth is a widely held belief that is untrue or may not always be true. If there are exceptions to a statement, even though it is popularly held to be true, it is a myth. We develop ideas about how we should act or not act sexually based on many influences, including ideas that are myths.

One example of a sexual myth many teens believe is that everyone is having sex. This belief is obviously a myth, yet it can cause teens to feel pressure to become or to continue to be sexually active.

Many myths develop as a result of media depictions of sex as always ideal, romantic, sensual, loving and joyous. Though this can certainly be true in the right setting, with the right person and at the right time of life, it is not always true. A teen's desire for this vision, along with the need to belong and be accepted, causes this myth to be accepted as the truth.

(continued...)

Sexuality and Myths

Instant Expert

Believing in sexual myths can result in sexual activity that proves harmful to teens and, therefore, to society. Damage to an individual's self-concept, relationships, health and future can be significant when a teen becomes sexually active at the wrong time in his or her life. Society also pays the cost of these problems in the form of medical and welfare costs for the teen pregnancies, sexually transmitted disease and social problems that may result.

Recognizing a statement as a myth can reduce the influence it has on a person, thereby increasing the chances that the person will make sounder decisions about sex.

Common Sexual Myths

Commonly believed myths about sex and sexuality include:

1. Having sex shows a couple is really in love.
2. Most teens are sexually active.
3. If a person has had sex once, there's no reason to say no to having sex again.
4. Boys need to have sex more than girls.
5. One way to keep a boyfriend or girlfriend is to have sex.
6. The best way to get to know someone is to have sex with him or her.
7. Having sex will make a relationship better.
8. Teens who are still virgins when graduating from high school are probably gay or lesbian.

Dimensions of Sexuality

Key

Biological

- *physical appearance*
- *growth and development*
- *sexual characteristics*
- *sexual desire and response*
- *ability to reproduce*

Biological is often thought of as the only dimension of sexuality. But it is only 1 of the 4. Biological functions are a natural part of being human.

Psychological

- *attitudes about self and others*
- *emotions*
- *life experiences*
- *motivation to act*
- *expressiveness*
- *learned behavior*

Our attitudes and feelings about ourselves as sexual beings are developed beginning very early in life. We are continuously told how to think and act as we experience our sexual development. This influences how we see and accept ourselves as sexual beings.

Sexuality

Cultural

- *family*
- *neighbors*
- *peers*
- *religious expression*
- *school*
- *dating habits*
- *laws*
- *advertising*
- *media*

Our culture, both historical and current, affects our thoughts and actions. Gender roles, sexual customs and laws, and the models we see around us are all functions of culture.

Ethical

- *family's values*
- *religious beliefs*
- *accepted morals*
- *personal values*

Concepts of right and wrong developed from several sources in our lives make up the ethical dimension of our sexuality.

UNIT

2

A World of Pressure

TIME

3–4 periods

ACTIVITIES:

1. Recognizing Pressure
2. Types of Pressure
3. Media Pressures
4. Analyzing Media Influences
5. Stereotypes and Pressures
6. Pressure for Sexual Responsibility
7. Media Messages

UNIT

2

A World of Pressure

OBJECTIVES

Students will be able to:

1. Identify both internal and external pressures to be sexually active.
2. Identify media sources of sexual pressure and their effects on teens.
3. Identify influences for sexual responsibility, or abstinence.

GETTING STARTED

Have:

- butcher paper
- markers
- art supplies

Copy for each student:

- Sexuality Pressures (2.1)
- Media Research Observation Form (2.4)
- Stereotypes of Males and Females (2.5)
- Media Messages—Family Page (2.7)
- Media Messages—Student Page (2.8)
- Media Messages—Feedback Form (2.9)
- Identifying Pressures (2.10)

Copy 1 for each group:

- Media Analysis Project (2.2)
- Media Influence Report (2.3)

Make transparency of:

- Stereotype (2.6)

SPECIAL STEPS

Gather magazines or record a video clip to demonstrate use of sex in the media. See Activity 3 (p. 23).

Make name cards for panel discussion. See Activity 4 (p. 24).

UNIT OVERVIEW

PURPOSE

Many factors, both internal and external, drive teens toward sexual activity. Some of the external factors include myths (as discussed in Unit 1), peer pressure, stereotypes and the many forms of media. Internal pressures include physical sexual desire, being in love, and needing acceptance and closeness.

Understanding these pressures and identifying which are most influential on an individual level helps teens learn to resist them. There are also factors that influence teens to choose sexual responsibility, or abstinence. Identifying these factors alongside of the pressures to be sexually active will help students prepare to make decisions about sexual expression that are best for them.

MAIN POINTS

- Awareness of the external and internal pressures to be sexually active increases the ability to resist these influences.
- Identifying factors that support choosing sexual responsibility, or abstinence, can encourage teens in their decision-making process.

REVIEW

To increase your understanding of internal and external influences on sexual activity, review **A World of Pressure** ***Instant Expert*** (p. 33).

VOCABULARY

analysis—The process of studying something to determine its features and relationships.

external pressure—Pressure from outside sources, e.g., family, peers, society.

internal pressure—Pressure from inside sources, e.g., personal beliefs, thoughts, attitudes.

media—All the means of communication that provide the public with news and entertainment, including newspapers, radio and TV.

pressure—Strong influence.

stereotype—Standardized image.

target audience—The group for whom a particular message is intended.

1. Recognizing Pressure

A Class Discussion Activity

MEETING STUDENT NEEDS

Review the groundrules before class discussion. Emphasize the importance of creating a respectful, "safe" environment in this class.

Discuss factors in decisions

Ask students to think of something they did recently where they had to think about the options and make a choice. Examples:

- what to wear to school
- whom to sit by in class
- what to eat for lunch

Ask students to identify some of the factors they considered to make that choice. Possible factors:

- their personal preferences
- concern about what others might think or do in response
- their feelings about others' potential reactions

Discuss pressures that influence decisions

Ask students for examples of pressures that could cause them to make choices that are not good for them. Examples:

- You eat pizza and fries for lunch because your friends tease you when you bring low-fat foods.
- Someone wears a T-shirt that some people find offensive because the group he/she wants to be in thinks it is cool.
- A boyfriend or girlfriend wants you to go further sexually than you feel ready for and you are afraid of losing him/her if you say no.

Point out that some pressures are very subtle and we may have a hard time recognizing them. Suggest that it is important to consider all of the types of pressures that influence decisions about sex so that we can control them and be able to act in ways that are healthful.

2. Types of Pressure

A Brainstorming and Self-Assessment Activity

Discuss types of pressures

Discuss external and internal pressures, using the **A World of Pressure** ***Instant Expert*** as a guide. Ask students to share some specific examples of internal and external pressures they know about or have seen.

Brainstorm internal and external pressures

Conduct a brainstorming session to generate a class list of possible internal and external pressures that influence teens to become sexually active. Write responses in 2 columns on the board, identifying them as "internal" or "external" pressures.

(continued...)

MATERIALS

- Sexuality Pressures (2.1)

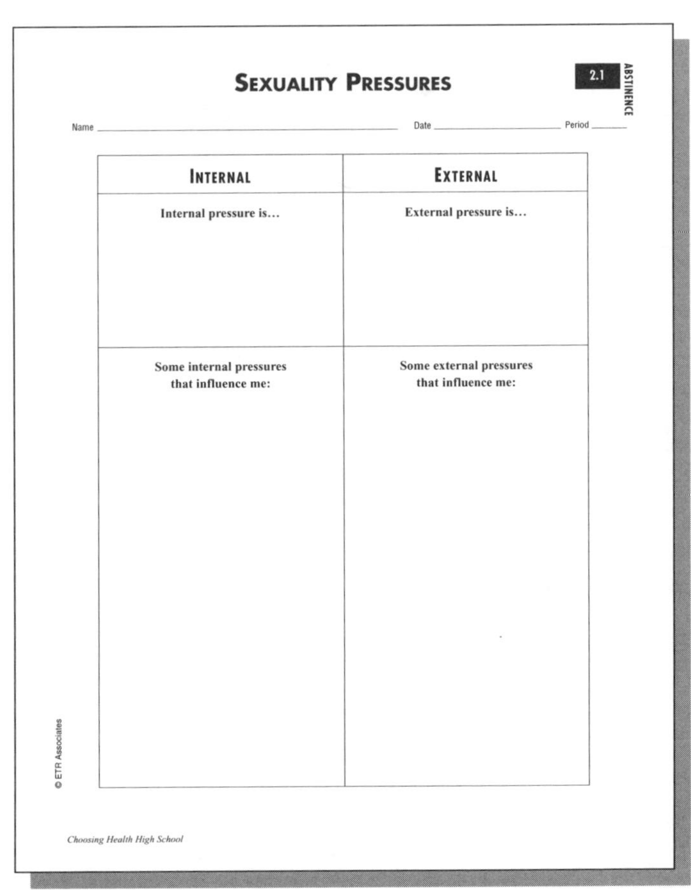

Sexuality Pressures 2.1 ABSTINENCE

Name ______ Date ______ Period ______

Internal	External
Internal pressure is...	External pressure is...
Some internal pressures that influence me:	Some external pressures that influence me:

© ETR Associates

Choosing Health High School

2. Types of Pressure

Continued

MEETING STUDENT NEEDS

Allow students to maintain privacy on the **Sexuality Pressures** activity sheet. Student responses should not be collected or shared with the class, but kept private for students' personal learning.

Students identify pressures

Distribute the **Sexuality Pressures** activity sheet. Have students write a definition of internal pressure at the top of one column and external pressure at the top of the other.

Then ask students to begin a private list of things that influence their own decisions about sex. They can begin by selecting some from the class list just created and then add others they are aware of. Allow time for students to work on this list individually and privately. Tell them that they will have opportunities to add to their lists in future lessons.

Ongoing Assessment Observe the accuracy and depth of student responses in brainstorming examples of internal and external pressures. See the **A World of Pressure** ***Instant Expert*** for assessment criteria.

Observe student work on the **Sexuality Pressures** activity sheet by walking around the room to see if students are able to identify items in both categories. Do not collect these activity sheets.

3. Media Pressures

A Class Discussion Activity

MATERIALS

- magazines or video clip

Brainstorm forms of media

Conduct a brainstorming session to identify the different forms of media that come into our lives. Be sure responses include:

- print media (newspapers and magazines)
- TV programs and commercials
- radio
- movies and videos
- music and music videos
- billboard advertising

Discuss media influences

Discuss the reasons media are such big business. Ask students: How much influence do media have on our actions?

Discuss how the media use sex to get our attention. Show a few examples from magazines or a short video clip from a popular movie or TV program. Ask students to describe examples they have seen of the use of sex in various media. What messages do they think these portrayals send to teens?

4. Analyzing Media Influences

A Media Analysis Activity

40 minutes, plus time for groups to prepare presentations

MATERIALS

- Media Analysis Project (2.2)
- Media Influence Report (2.3)
- Media Research Observation Form (2.4)
- art supplies
- Name Cards for panel presentation
- Sexuality Pressures (2.1), from Activity 2

MEETING STUDENT NEEDS

Forming cooperative groups for this project will require a blending of student talents in each group. You may want to form groups based on students' recognition of their own talents as reporters, artists, writers or researchers. Be considerate of those students who will need more direction to accomplish the task. Check each group as it begins the project to see that individual assignments are appropriately made.

Groups analyze media influences

Divide the class into 6 groups, and assign a different media—print, TV, radio, movies, music or billboards—to each group for analysis.

Give each group a copy of the **Media Analysis Project** and the **Media Influence Report** activity sheets. Give each student a copy of the **Media Research Observation Form**. Explain the group assignment:

- Choose a research director, an art director, a writer and a reporter. You may want to share a few of the roles if there are more than 4 people in your group.
- Read the directions on the **Media Analysis Project** activity sheet for designing the research process, gathering evidence and creating a presentation.
- Each member of the group will complete a **Media Research Observation Form**.
- Complete the activities and prepare your presentation and the materials to be turned in.
- Writers will complete the **Media Influence Report** activity sheet.
- Art directors will create the poster to show the group's evidence.
- Reporters will present group findings as part of a panel discussion.

(continued...)

NAME CARDS

Prepare Name Cards for the panel discussion. Write the name of each media group on a piece of heavy paper that can be set in front of panel members. Use the following groups:

- Newspapers and Magazines
- TV Programs and Commercials
- Radio
- Movies and Videos
- Music and Music Videos
- Billboard Advertising

4. Analyzing Media Influences

Continued

Conduct panel discussion

Choose a student to act as moderator for the panel discussion or moderate the panel yourself. Have the reporter from each group join the panel at the table at the front of the room. Place a Name Card indicating which media the panel member represents in front of each person.

Begin the panel discussion by asking reporters to present their group's posters of evidence. Post these on the wall behind the panel.

Have the moderator ask the questions from the **Media Influence Report** activity sheet. Allow each reporter to answer the question before going on to the next question. After the presentation, allow the class to ask questions of the reporters.

(continued...)

COMMUNITY LINK

Hang group posters in the school library, hallway or other public area, or arrange a display describing the project and highlighting group posters at the public library or other community center.

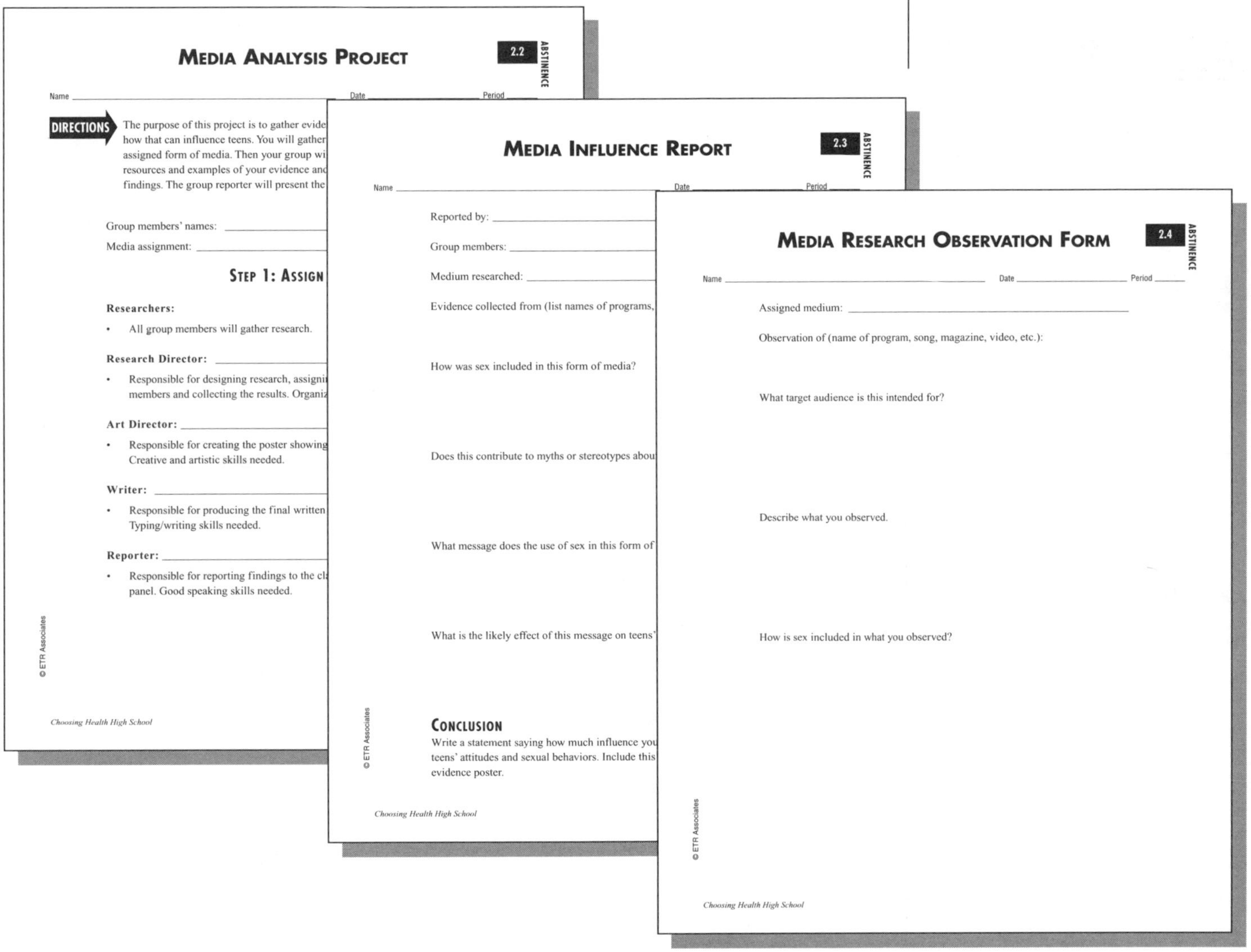

Media Analysis Project 2.2 ABSTINENCE

Name ______ Date ______ Period ______

DIRECTIONS The purpose of this project is to gather evide how that can influence teens. You will gather assigned form of media. Then your group wi resources and examples of your evidence and findings. The group reporter will present the

Group members' names: ______

Media assignment: ______

Step 1: Assign

Researchers:

- All group members will gather research.

Research Director: ______

- Responsible for designing research, assigni members and collecting the results. Organiz

Art Director: ______

- Responsible for creating the poster showing Creative and artistic skills needed.

Writer: ______

- Responsible for producing the final written Typing/writing skills needed.

Reporter: ______

- Responsible for reporting findings to the cl panel. Good speaking skills needed.

© ETR Associates

Choosing Health High School

Media Influence Report 2.3 ABSTINENCE

Name ______ Date ______ Period ______

Reported by: ______

Group members: ______

Medium researched: ______

Evidence collected from (list names of programs,

How was sex included in this form of media?

Does this contribute to myths or stereotypes abou

What message does the use of sex in this form of

What is the likely effect of this message on teens

Conclusion

Write a statement saying how much influence yo teens' attitudes and sexual behaviors. Include this evidence poster.

© ETR Associates

Choosing Health High School

Media Research Observation Form 2.4 ABSTINENCE

Name ______ Date ______ Period ______

Assigned medium: ______

Observation of (name of program, song, magazine, video, etc.):

What target audience is this intended for?

Describe what you observed.

How is sex included in what you observed?

© ETR Associates

Choosing Health High School

EXTEND THE LEARNING

Invite the social studies or psychology teacher and/or class to be guests for the presentations. Invite them to join in the question-and-answer period.

After the panel discussion, as a class, have students prepare a graph to report the results of the media research, comparing the incidence of sex per amount of time in each media.

Students add to list of pressures

Ask students to add to their list of internal and external pressures on the **Sexuality Pressures** activity sheet from Activity 2.

Ongoing Assessment Assess students' work on the **Media Influence Report** and **Media Research Observation Form** activity sheets and on group posters for the completeness of their observations, the thoroughness of the research and the amount of evidence provided.

As students add to the list on the **Sexuality Pressures** activity sheet, walk around the room and observe their ability to identify influences from media sources. Remember that this is a private list of personal influences.

5. Stereotypes and Pressures

A Class Discussion and Brainstorming Activity

Define stereotype

Distribute the **Stereotypes of Males and Females** activity sheet. Ask students to define a stereotype. Display the **Stereotype** transparency with the definition covered. Uncover and read the definition and discuss it with students. Ask students to write the definition on the activity sheet.

Discuss typical stereotypes

Uncover the heading "Typical Stereotypes" on the **Stereotype** transparency. Ask students to brainstorm a list of typical stereotypes for males and for females. Write these on the transparency in the appropriate columns.

Then review the lists with students. Strive for a general class consensus on the stereotypes for males and females.

Ask students to select 3 stereotypes from the list of male stereotypes and 3 from the list of female stereotypes that they think are most obvious in their community. Have them write the stereotypes they select on the activity sheet.

(continued...)

MATERIALS

- Stereotypes of Males and Females (2.5)
- Stereotype (2.6)
- Sexuality Pressures (2.1), from Activity 2

Stereotypes of Males and Females 2.5 ABSTINENCE

Name ______________________ Date ____________ Period ______

Definition of stereotype:

Typical stereotypes:	
Men	**Women**

Sexual stereotypes that cause the most pressure for teens:

Choosing Health High School

Stereotype 2.6 ABSTINENCE

Definition: A standard image of what a person should be or do.

Typical Stereotypes:	
Men	**Women**

Sexual stereotypes that could cause pressure toward sexual activity:

Choosing Health High School

5. Stereotypes and Pressures

Continued

> **MEETING STUDENT NEEDS**
>
> Be sensitive to the various cultures in the community. Balance the stereotypes presented to represent all cultures equally.
>
> In the discussion of sexual stereotypes, be sensitive to students who may be questioning their sexual orientation or who may identify as gay or lesbian. One way to do this is to refer to a "dating partner" or "someone they date" when discussing stereotypical expectations of boys and girls.
>
> 

Discuss sexual stereotypes

Write this stereotype on the board: All boys want (from girls) is sex. Discuss whether this stereotype is really true or a myth. Ask students:

- Is this a stereotype that many boys try to live up to, at least in the way they talk?
- What happens when boys think they have to live up to this stereotype?
- Are they likely to do or say things that they don't really mean or aren't really true?
- Can this pressure be hard for boys to deal with?

Write this stereotype on the board: It's the girl's responsibility to say no to sex. Discuss whether this stereotype is true. Ask students:

- Does this stereotype place a lot of pressure on girls?
- Does it perhaps remove some responsibility from boys that they should share?
- What happens when girls think they have to live up to this stereotype?
- Can this stereotype lead to actions that aren't healthful?

Brainstorm sexual stereotypes

Conduct a brainstorming session to identify sexual stereotypes for males and females that could cause pressure toward sexual activity. Write responses on the **Stereotype** transparency or on the board.

Discuss the possible pressure from each stereotype listed. What behaviors could be the result? Ask students to choose 3–5 stereotypes that they believe cause the most pressure toward sexual activity and to write these stereotypes on the activity sheet.

Students add to list of pressures

Ask students to add to their list of internal and external pressures on the **Sexuality Pressures** activity sheet from Activity 2.

Ongoing Assessment Ask students to write a response on the back of the activity sheet to this question: Do sexual stereotypes make it easier or harder to make good decisions about sexual activity? How?

Assess students' responses on the **Stereotypes of Males and Females** activity sheet for the following elements:

- Do the typical stereotypes that students selected as most common in their community seem consistent with the community?
- Do the sexual stereotypes students chose as causing most pressure for teens reflect understanding of the concept?
- Do students' responses to the assessment question identify the fact that many stereotypes about males and females are myths and can cause a great deal of pressure to act in ways that might be harmful?

6. Pressure for Sexual Responsibility

A Small Group Activity

40 minutes

✷

MATERIALS

- butcher paper
- markers
- Sexuality Pressures (2.1), from Activity 2

MEETING STUDENT NEEDS

Some students may find it difficult to develop this list with a partner. You may need to begin the activity with groups of 3, then join 2 groups to make the group of 6 for the final step.

EXTEND THE LEARNING

Survey the class to identify the most commonly cited sexual stereotypes of males and females. Students can develop a plan to change these stereotypes to reduce their influence on teens. Encourage students to conduct library research and interviews with local authorities. Students can write a class paper to present to school and community leaders.

Dyads identify influences for sexual responsibility

Tell students that there are also many factors in their lives that influence them to practice sexual responsibility—such as choosing abstinence until they feel ready for sex. Discuss a few examples of these factors, using **A World of Pressure** ***Instant Expert*** as a guide.

Ask students to work with a partner of their choice to make a list of additional factors that can influence teens to practice abstinence.

Groups combine lists

After 4–5 minutes, have dyads combine into groups of 6. Distribute butcher paper and markers and explain the group assignment:

- Combine your dyad lists into 1 group list.
- Write this group list on butcher paper under the title "Influences for Sexual Responsibility."

Groups report

Have groups post their lists on the wall and share with the class. Allow students to add other factors as identified. Correct any misconceptions and fill in any additional influences for sexual responsibility not covered by group lists, using **A World of Pressure** ***Instant Expert*** as a guide.

Ongoing Assessment Ask students to take out their **Sexuality Pressures** activity sheet from Activity 2 once more. Have them draw a line under the last entry in each column and then add the influences for sexual responsibility presented by the groups, placing them in the correct column: internal or external. Observe students' ability to identify the influences correctly.

7. Media Messages

A Family Discussion Activity

5 minutes, plus follow-up

✷

MATERIALS

- Media Messages—Family Page (2.7)
- Media Messages—Student Page (2.8)
- Media Messages—Feedback Form (2.9)

Initiate family activity

Distribute the **Media Messages—Family Page, Student Page** and **Feedback Form.** Ask students to take the activity sheets home and complete this assignment with their parents or other adult family members.

(continued...)

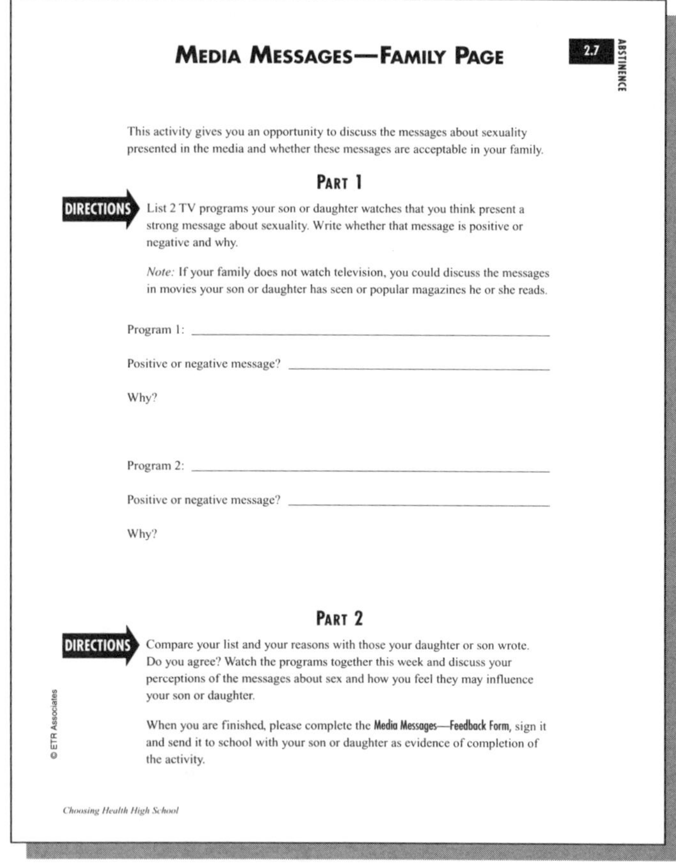

MEDIA MESSAGES—FAMILY PAGE 2.7 ABSTINENCE

This activity gives you an opportunity to discuss the messages about sexuality presented in the media and whether these messages are acceptable in your family.

PART 1

DIRECTIONS List 2 TV programs your son or daughter watches that you think present a strong message about sexuality. Write whether that message is positive or negative and why.

Note: If your family does not watch television, you could discuss the messages in movies your son or daughter has seen or popular magazines he or she reads.

Program 1: ____________________

Positive or negative message? ____________________

Why?

Program 2: ____________________

Positive or negative message? ____________________

Why?

PART 2

DIRECTIONS Compare your list and your reasons with those your daughter or son wrote. Do you agree? Watch the programs together this week and discuss your perceptions of the messages about sex and how you feel they may influence your son or daughter.

When you are finished, please complete the **Media Messages—Feedback Form**, sign it and send it to school with your son or daughter as evidence of completion of the activity.

© ETR Associates

Choosing Health High School

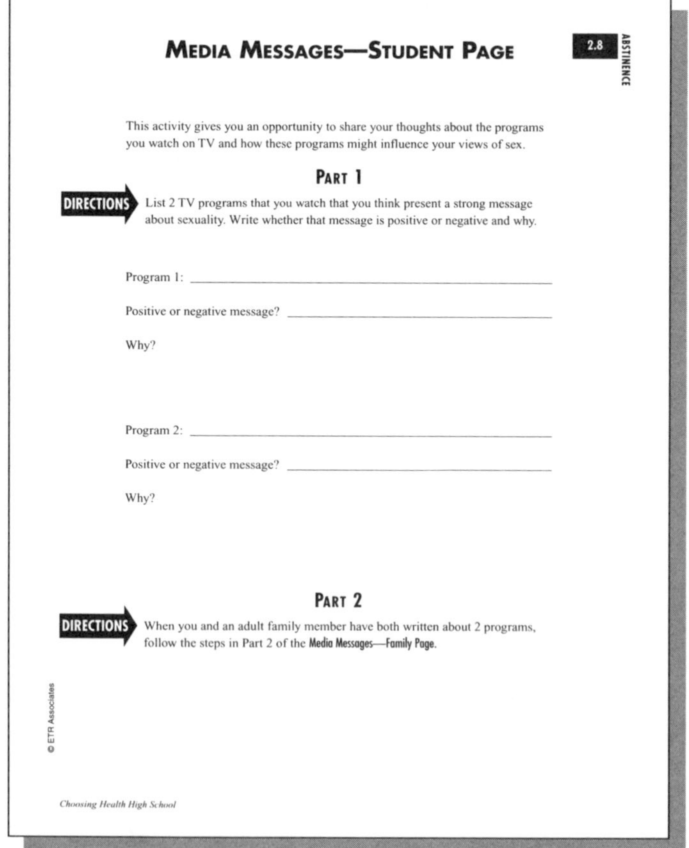

MEDIA MESSAGES—STUDENT PAGE 2.8 ABSTINENCE

This activity gives you an opportunity to share your thoughts about the programs you watch on TV and how these programs might influence your views of sex.

PART 1

DIRECTIONS List 2 TV programs that you watch that you think present a strong message about sexuality. Write whether that message is positive or negative and why.

Program 1: ____________________

Positive or negative message? ____________________

Why?

Program 2: ____________________

Positive or negative message? ____________________

Why?

PART 2

DIRECTIONS When you and an adult family member have both written about 2 programs, follow the steps in Part 2 of the **Media Messages—Family Page.**

© ETR Associates

Choosing Health High School

Continued

Discuss family activity

Ask students to discuss the family activity in general terms. Ask students:

- Did you find more positive or more negative messages in the programs you watched?
- In general, did you agree or disagree with your parent about the sexuality messages presented in the programs?
- How was it to watch the programs with your family? Did this shared viewing give you any new perceptions?

Collect the **Feedback Forms** to give students credit for completing the assignment.

MEETING STUDENT NEEDS

If students do not have a television at home, they can discuss the messages in movies they have seen or popular magazines they read.

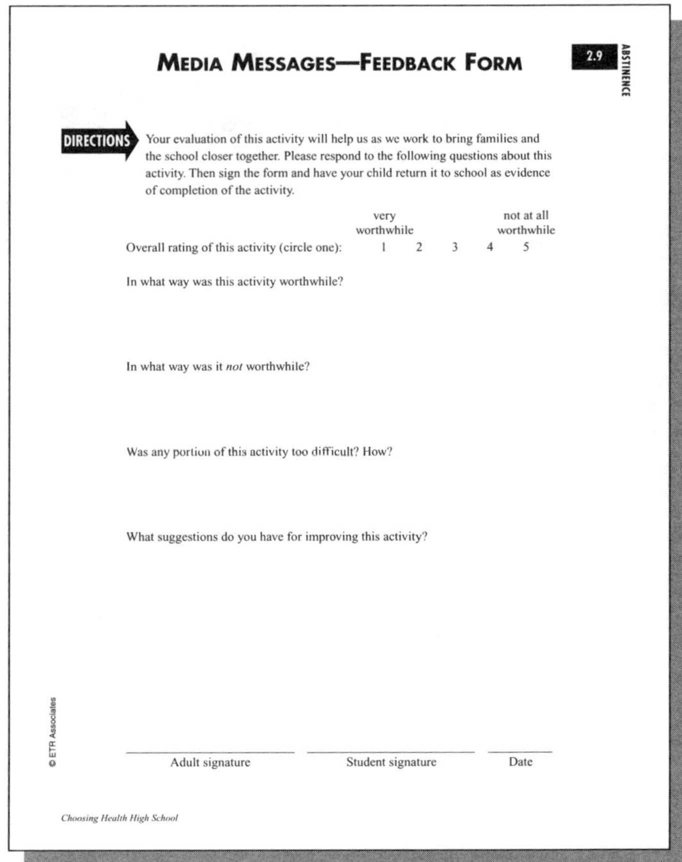

Media Messages—Feedback Form

2.9 ABSTINENCE

DIRECTIONS Your evaluation of this activity will help us as we work to bring families and the school closer together. Please respond to the following questions about this activity. Then sign the form and have your child return it to school as evidence of completion of the activity.

	very worthwhile				not at all worthwhile
Overall rating of this activity (circle one):	1	2	3	4	5

In what way was this activity worthwhile?

In what way was it *not* worthwhile?

Was any portion of this activity too difficult? How?

What suggestions do you have for improving this activity?

Adult signature ____ Student signature ____ Date ____

Choosing Health High School

EVALUATION

20 minutes

REVIEW

- A World of Pressure *Instant Expert* (p. 33)

MATERIALS

- Identifying Pressures (2.10)

✷

OBJECTIVES

Students will be able to:

1. **Identify both internal and external pressures to be sexually active.**
2. **Identify media sources of sexual pressure and their effects on teens.**
3. **Identify influences for sexual responsibility, or abstinence.**

Distribute the **Identifying Pressures** evaluation sheet and have students complete it. Ask for volunteers to share their answers.

CRITERIA

Review students' responses on the **Identifying Pressures** evaluation sheet for:

- identification of truly significant pressures that teens face
- correct identification of internal and external pressures
- evidence of value for sexual responsibility and creativity in suggestions

See the **A World of Pressure *Instant Expert*** for evaluation criteria.

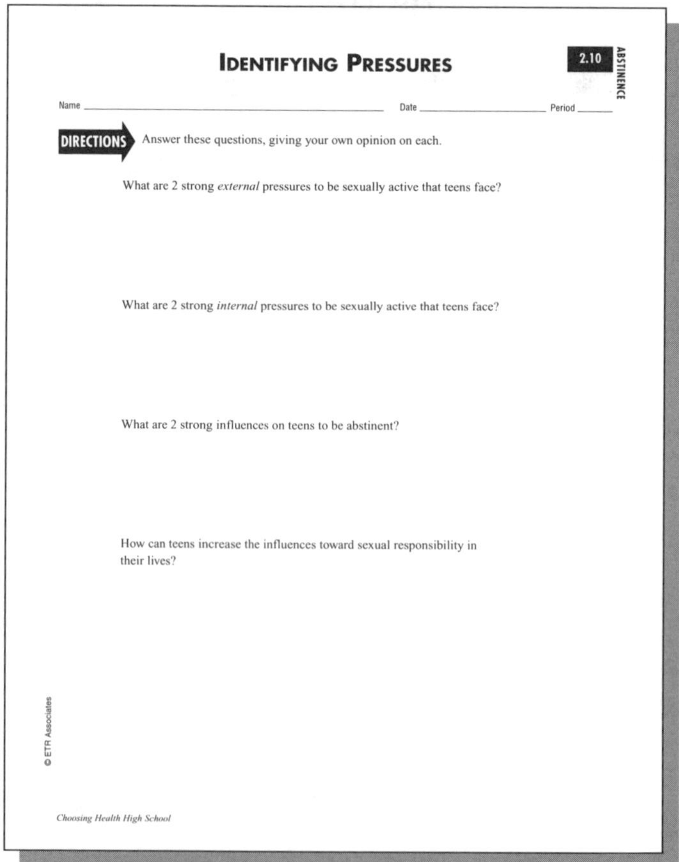

IDENTIFYING PRESSURES 2.10 ABSTINENCE

Name ______________ Date ______________ Period ______

DIRECTIONS Answer these questions, giving your own opinion on each.

What are 2 strong *external* pressures to be sexually active that teens face?

What are 2 strong *internal* pressures to be sexually active that teens face?

What are 2 strong influences on teens to be abstinent?

How can teens increase the influences toward sexual responsibility in their lives?

© ETR Associates

Choosing Health High School

A World of Pressure

Instant Expert

Teens today face many pressures, particularly pressures to be sexually active. Pressures may be either internal or external in source and may work as positive as well as negative influences.

INTERNAL AND EXTERNAL INFLUENCES

Pressures to be sexually active can come from within us. They develop in response to certain needs, such as the need to be loved and accepted, the need to express love, the physical desire for sexual intimacy or pleasure, or curiosity.

These needs can be met in many ways that are not sexual. But if they are not met, they become stronger and may make sexual activity seem even more appealing. Recognizing that these internal pressures exist and that they can be very influential is an important step in controlling our response to them.

External pressures to be sexually active come from other people and society. Myths are one source of external pressure. Peers, families, the media and common sexual stereotypes are other sources of external pressures. These external pressures are everywhere. They often seem to promote sexual activity as desirable and acceptable for teens. Examining these influences will help teens put them into perspective and make considered, careful decisions about sex.

MEDIA INFLUENCES

The media have a strong influence in the lives of most people. Media reinforce many of the internal and external drives for sexual activity. They can make myths about sex seem true and sexual stereotypes seem real. Teens are exposed to many forms of media on a daily basis, including television programs and commercials; print media in newspapers, tabloids and magazines; radio programming and commercials; movies and videos; music and music videos; and billboard and store advertising.

Media messages are everywhere and continual. All of us, especially teens, are exposed to sexual suggestion in the media in staggering amounts. No wonder sex is such a big concern.

That sex happens quickly, easily and is a goal of relationships is one of the most common media themes. The message to teens is that sex is good and carries few consequences. Though it is true that sex is a natural part of a healthy life, it is not always OK for teens. It can, in fact, cause many problems, which the media usually fail to depict.

(continued...)

A World of Pressure

INSTANT EXPERT

SEXUAL STEREOTYPES

Stereotypes are standard images of what a person should be or do that are accepted by a group. The accepted stereotype often influences the actions of those in the group. It becomes the goal or ideal to be measured against.

Stereotypes can be helpful when they give us a model of what is expected that we can live up to and be guided by. However, more often they cause problems, because they tend to limit people and pressure them into actions that may not really be right for them. Stereotypes about sex can cause a great deal of pressure on teens, influencing their behavior in ways that are not always positive.

Stereotypes of males and females can lead us to act in certain ways and treat others with less concern for individuals and their unique needs and abilities. When teens believe these stereotypes, they may be influenced to become sexually active. Placing certain expectations on young people may cause them to feel less self-confident about themselves and their decisions.

Examples of common stereotypes for men include:

- Men don't have feelings.
- All men want from women is sex.
- Men are more knowledgeable and experienced sexually.
- Men *need* sex.

Examples of common stereotypes for women include:

- It's the woman's role to say *no.*
- It's the woman's responsibility to use protection.
- Women dress to tease men.
- Saying no doesn't really mean no.

(continued…)

A World of Pressure

Instant Expert

PRESSURE *FOR* SEXUAL RESPONSIBILITY AND ABSTINENCE

Although many pressures push teens to consider becoming sexually active, there are also influences for teens to remain abstinent. These influences are not as obvious to teens, and may be mixed with those that encourage sexual activity, creating the confusion that makes this such a difficult subject.

When teens can identify positive influences toward sexual responsibility in their lives and assess the personal relevance and importance of these influences, the "Should I or shouldn't I?" question becomes easier to address. Many teens have not clearly identified these other influences and, therefore, cannot see how they counter media messages and stereotypes. If the influences for becoming sexually active appear stronger, teens are more likely to make that decision.

The influences that encourage teens to choose abstinence include:

- family values
- religious values
- goals for the future
- physical health—avoidance of disease and pregnancy
- quality of relationship
- self-respect that comes from following their true beliefs and feelings

Teens need to be encouraged to consider how all of these influences around sexual activity affect them personally. They need to understand how influences can be either positive or negative. Recognizing positive influences for abstinence and sexual responsibility can help teens make more informed decisions that will protect their emotional and physical health.

UNIT

3

RISKS AND DECISIONS

TIME

3 periods

ACTIVITIES

1. Risk and Reward
2. Temptation and Self-Control
3. Making Decisions
4. Controlling Impulses
5. Are You Ready for Sex?

UNIT

3

Risks and Decisions

OBJECTIVE

Students will be able to:

1. Describe the influence of risk-taking behavior on sexual decision making.

2. Apply the decision-making process and STAR method to examples of situations of sexual temptation.

GETTING STARTED

Have:

- posterboard or butcher paper
- scissors
- tape or glue

Copy 1 for each group:

- Thrill Seekers List (3.1)

Copy for each student:

- Temptations (3.2)
- Decision-Making Steps (3.4)
- STAR Cartoon (3.6)
- Are You Ready for Sex?—Family Page (3.8)
- Are You Ready for Sex?—Student Page (3.9)
- Are You Ready for Sex?—Feedback Form (3.10)
- Evaluating Risks and Decisions (3.11)

Make transparency of:

- 5 Steps in Decision Making (3.3)
- STAR (3.5)
- STAR Cartoon Example (3.7)

Unit Overview

PURPOSE

Taking risks is a natural part of life. Some "thrill seekers" are willing to take greater risks than others. Learning to look at a risk in terms of what it has to offer that we want (the reward) and what the result might be (the consequence) helps us make better decisions.

Students may not be ready to handle the consequences of being sexually active, yet temptations to become sexually active are all around them. Considering the risks and rewards of actions and identifying personal means of self-control will help teens make healthy decisions about sex.

MAIN POINTS

- Risks have both rewards and consequences that must be considered when making decisions.
- Temptations to be sexually active can lead to impulsive actions.
- Risks, rewards and consequences, and ways to increase self-control must be considered in making decisions about sexual activity.

REVIEW

To increase your understanding of risks and temptations, self-control and decision making, review **Risk Taking and Self-Control *Instant Expert*** (p. 50).

VOCABULARY

consequence—The result of an action.

decision—The act of making up one's mind.

reward—The benefit of taking a risk.

risk—The likelihood of injury, damage or other negative consequences following an action.

self-control—Ability to control behavior or expression of emotions.

temptation—The opportunity to do something risky.

1. Risk and Reward

A Class Discussion and Small Group Activity

MATERIALS

- Thrill Seekers List (3.1)
- posterboard or butcher paper
- scissors
- tape or glue

MEETING STUDENT NEEDS

Be cautious in discussing illegal actions as risks. You do not want to put students in a compromising position. You may want to review class groundrules before this discussion.

✷

Define risk

Ask students to raise their hands if they consider themselves risk takers. Explore what they mean by risk. Possible definition:

- Exposing oneself to possible injury or loss.

Ask for some examples of risks and write them on the board. Ask students:

- Are there degrees of risk?
- How many of you would take little risks? Why?
- How many of you like to take bigger risks? Why?

Discuss rewards and consequences

Ask students what makes a risk worth taking. Discuss the 3 components of risk taking—risks, rewards and consequences—using the **Risk Taking and Self-Control *Instant Expert*** as a guide. Offer students an example:

- **Risk:** Jumping off a cliff into the water.
- **Reward:** The thrill of the action and impressing others.
- **Consequence:** A broken leg (if the water isn't deep enough).

(continued...)

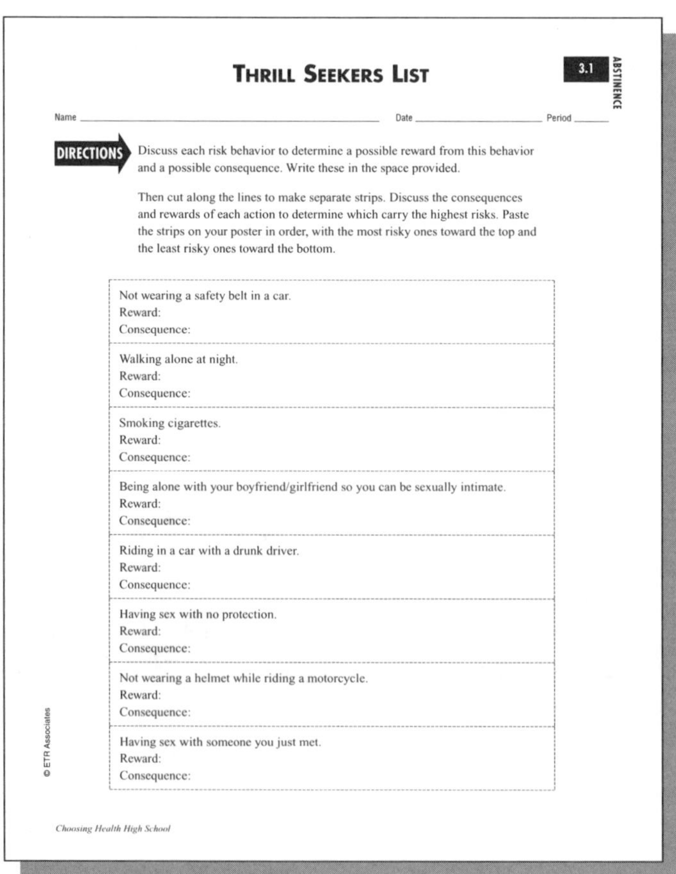

Thrill Seekers List

3.1 ABSTINENCE

Name ______ Date ______ Period ______

DIRECTIONS Discuss each risk behavior to determine a possible reward from this behavior and a possible consequence. Write these in the space provided.

Then cut along the lines to make separate strips. Discuss the consequences and rewards of each action to determine which carry the highest risks. Paste the strips on your poster in order, with the most risky ones toward the top and the least risky ones toward the bottom.

Not wearing a safety belt in a car.
Reward:
Consequence:

Walking alone at night.
Reward:
Consequence:

Smoking cigarettes.
Reward:
Consequence:

Being alone with your boyfriend/girlfriend so you can be sexually intimate.
Reward:
Consequence:

Riding in a car with a drunk driver.
Reward:
Consequence:

Having sex with no protection.
Reward:
Consequence:

Not wearing a helmet while riding a motorcycle.
Reward:
Consequence:

Having sex with someone you just met.
Reward:
Consequence:

Choosing Health High School

1. Risk and Reward

Continued

Look at the examples of risk on the board. List what the reward might be for each one. Now list some possible consequences of each action. Ask students to consider how the consequences and risks balance. Are the risks worth it?

Groups create posters

Divide the class into groups of 4 or 5. Give each group posterboard or a large piece of paper (approximately 11" x 17") and 1 copy of the **Thrill Seekers List** activity sheet. Explain the group assignment:

- Discuss each risk behavior on the **Thrill Seekers List.**
- Decide what the reward for the behavior might be and what a possible consequence might be. Write these in the space provided.
- Cut on the lines to separate each behavior.
- Discuss the balance between the reward and consequence of each behavior.
- Label the top of the poster "Most Risk." Label the bottom "Least Risk."
- Create a risk continuum by pasting the behaviors from the **Thrill Seekers List** activity sheet on the poster in order from the most to the least risky.

Discuss posters

Ask students to name some of the factors that influenced their assessment of the risk of each behavior. Possible responses:

- whether they have actually tried the behavior before
- whether the consequences were good or bad
- if the good consequences (rewards) were greater than the bad ones
- if they have been told about this experience by someone they respect
- if they could take the risk without the possibility of permanent consequences

Ask groups to share their completed posters with the class. Discuss how the groups decided which behaviors were most risky. Display the posters in the classroom for a few days.

Ongoing Assessment Review posters to assess students' comprehension of the concepts of reward and consequence. Look for the choice of most to least risky to reflect knowledge of the potential of each action to cause harm. Placement of the behaviors from high to low should reflect an understanding of the balance of risk to reward.

FAMILY LINK

Give each student a copy of the **Thrill Seekers List** activity sheet. Ask students to take the list home and find out how their families would rank these risks. Encourage students to compare family rankings to the group rankings and discuss any differences.

EXTEND THE LEARNING

Students can create a chart or graph showing the rank order of these risks from high to low as averaged from the groups' posters.

2. Temptation and Self-Control

A Roleplay Activity

50 minutes

MATERIALS

- Temptations (3.2)

✱

EXTEND THE LEARNING

Suggest that students keep a daily log for 3–5 days in which they record any temptations they encounter that challenge their personal rules. They might include information such as: day, location, with whom, tempted by, how they responded, and the results (positive or negative). They can then review the situation and suggest other ways to have handled it. At the end of the time, ask students to summarize the temptations faced and how well they handled them.

Discuss temptations

Ask students to share some examples of temptations to act in risky ways that teens might face. Discuss temptations to act sexually, using the **Risk Taking and Self-Control *Instant Expert*** as a guide.

Brainstorm benefits of abstinence

Ask students to list individually on a sheet of paper reasons to stay abstinent. Then create a class list on the board. Discuss benefits as they are listed.

Discuss self-control

Define self-control as the ability to follow our own rules. Ask students where self-control comes from. Discuss the development of self-control, using the **Risk Taking and Self-Control *Instant Expert*** as a guide.

(continued...)

Temptations — 3.2 Abstinence

Name ______ Date ______ Period ______

Situation	My Value	My "Rule"	Consequence	My Action
1. You don't know an answer on the math test, but you can see the answer sheet of Bill, the class "brain." (cheating)	Honesty	Do the best I can at the time.	If I cheat and get caught, I could flunk. Even if I don't get caught, I'll feel guilty.	Think as hard as I can. Do my best.
2. Megan is spreading rumors about you that have made you really angry. She says to meet her after school to "settle" things. (fighting)				
3. At a party, Danny gives you a beer and challenges you to chug it. (drinking)				
4. Chris and a group of friends are going to the park at noon. They say it's easy to cut class. (skipping class)				
5. Susie invites you to her room during a party. She says she wants to be alone with you. (sexual activity)				
6. Hal has invited you to go swimming at midnight when no one else will be around. (sexual activity)				
7. ______				

Choosing Health High School

2. Temptation and Self-Control

Continued

Students analyze temptations

Distribute the **Temptations** activity sheet. Review the first example with the class. Ask students to complete the remaining examples on their own. Encourage them to add other examples with which they might deal.

Students create roleplays

Ask students to work with 1 other person to develop a 1–2 minute roleplay demonstrating using self-control to respond to a temptation. They can choose a situation from the **Temptations** activity sheet or make up one of their own.

Have students share their roleplays with the class. Encourage students to share the personal rules that are the basis for their actions. Emphasize again that experience with using self-control to handle a temptation, even in roleplay, can help make it easier to act according to your own rules when you are tempted.

SHARPEN THE SKILL

ASSERTIVENESS—ARTICULATING PERSONAL BELIEFS

Making a public declaration of belief is considered an important aspect of establishing healthy behaviors. Ask students to share their rules by starting with the statement "I believe ______ (e.g., honesty) is important because…"

3. Making Decisions

A Class Discussion Activity

15 minutes

Materials

- transparency of 5 Steps in Decision Making (3.3)
- Decision-Making Steps (3.4)

Review decision-making skills

Display the **5 Steps in Decision Making** transparency and ask students to describe each step. Ask them to explain why each step is important to good decisions. Have students help you apply the steps to the decision to attend college (or another issue that is pertinent to your students) to demonstrate the use of each step.

List decisions

Ask students to help you make a list of real-life decisions they must make. Write these on the board. Guide students to include the decisions about sex that they face. Examples:

- How do you stick to a decision to be abstinent?
- What sort of sexual behaviors are OK for you (e.g., kissing, petting)?
- How do you handle pressure to have sex?
- When is it necessary to discuss protection from pregnancy and sexually transmitted disease?

(continued...)

5 Steps in Decision Making 3.3 ABSTINENCE

Decision to be made:

____

1. Gather **information.**
2. List possible **actions.**
3. List **consequences** of each action.
4. **Choose** the best action and try it.
5. **Evaluate** the outcome.

Choosing Health High School

3. Making Decisions

Continued

Students apply skills

Ask students to select 2 issues from the list of decisions that are most important for them at this time. Encourage students to examine a decision around sexual activity. Distribute the **Decision-Making Steps** activity sheet and have students work through the decision-making process for these 2 issues. Tell them to list 1 issue on each side.

Suggest students consider the following questions to assist in evaluating decisions about sex:

- Will I feel good about myself if I do this?
- Will the other person feel good about this experience and about me?

Ongoing Assessment Review the **Decision-Making Steps** activity sheet to see if the information provided is complete and matches each step of the process. The decision reached should be the logical result of the steps. Look for thorough consideration and logical development of the decision; do not judge the decision itself. Offer suggestions of other information to consider if necessary.

Sharpen the Skill

Decision Making—Top Ten List

An important part of the decision-making process is the recognition that a decision needs to be made. Have students create a "Top Ten" list of important decisions that typical teens face. Conduct a survey and post the results.

Decision-Making Steps 3.4 ABSTINENCE

Name ______ Date ______ Period ______

Decision to be made: ______

1. Information: ______

2. Actions: ______

3. Consequences: ______

4. Choose 1 action: ______

5. Evaluate: ______

© ETR Associates

Choosing Health High School

4. Controlling Impulses

An Artistic Expression Activity

30 minutes

MATERIALS

- transparency of STAR (3.5)
- STAR Cartoon (3.6)
- transparency of STAR Cartoon Example (3.7)

Discuss STAR

Display the **STAR** transparency. Explain that the STAR method is designed to help people **S**top, **T**hink, **A**ct and **R**eview an impulse before they take action. Review the steps on the **STAR** transparency.

Students practice STAR

Distribute the **STAR Cartoon** activity sheet and display the **STAR Cartoon Example** transparency. Review the example with students, pointing out the STAR steps and how they are used.

Ask students to think of a decision they have made. Tell them that the cartoon they will create should represent a situation where this decision is being questioned by another person. Ask them to draw the frames and fill in the dialog boxes to show what they would think to themselves and say to the other person as they used the STAR method.

Allow students to color their cartoons and add additional frames if they choose.

(continued...)

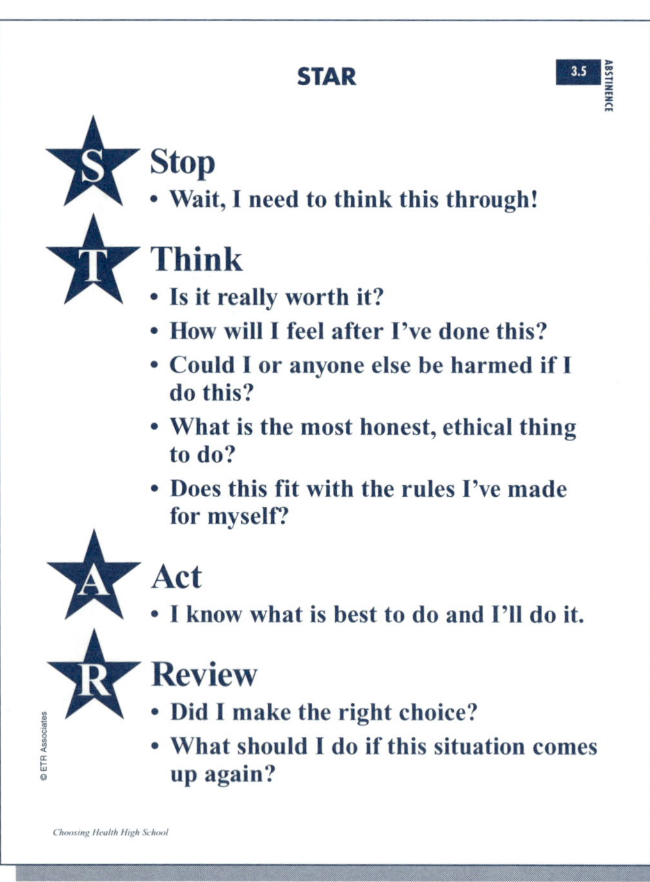

STAR 3.5 ABSTINENCE

S Stop
- Wait, I need to think this through!

T Think
- Is it really worth it?
- How will I feel after I've done this?
- Could I or anyone else be harmed if I do this?
- What is the most honest, ethical thing to do?
- Does this fit with the rules I've made for myself?

A Act
- I know what is best to do and I'll do it.

R Review
- Did I make the right choice?
- What should I do if this situation comes up again?

© ETR Associates

Choosing Health High School

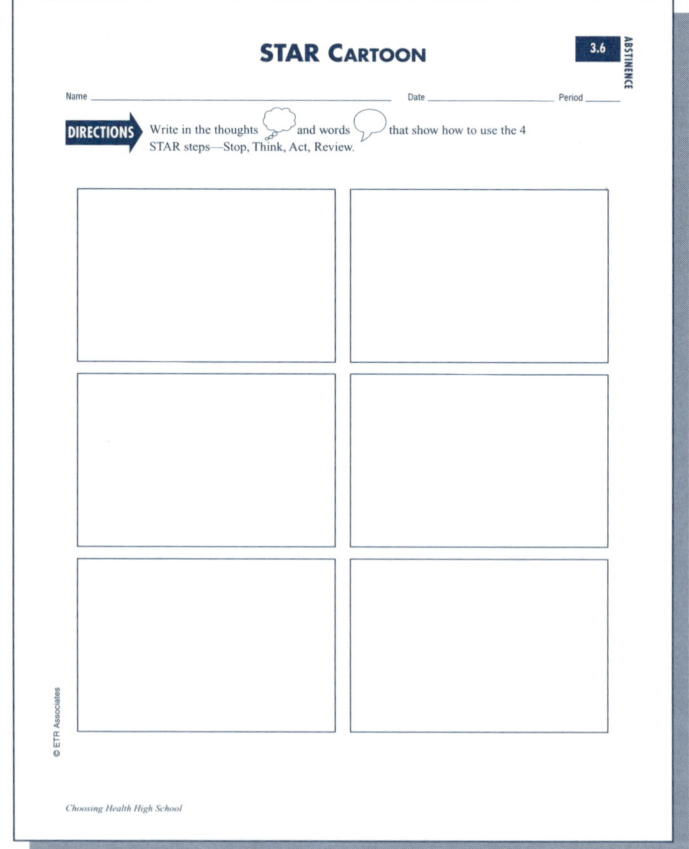

STAR Cartoon 3.6 ABSTINENCE

Name ______ Date ______ Period ______

DIRECTIONS Write in the thoughts and words that show how to use the 4 STAR steps—Stop, Think, Act, Review.

© ETR Associates

Choosing Health High School

4. Controlling Impulses

Continued

Students share cartoons

Ask for volunteers to share their **Star Cartoons** with the class. Collect and post the activity sheets.

Ongoing Assessment Review the STAR cartoons to see that each step of STAR is correctly reflected.

SHARPEN THE SKILL

DECISION MAKING—EVALUATING AND MAKING CHANGES

Challenge students to review their decisions after listening to the comments of the class. Would their decision change based on new information? Would it stay the same?

COMMUNITY LINK

Create a class book of the STAR cartoons. Share this with others by placing it on display in the library.

STAR Cartoon Example 3.7 ABSTINENCE

DIRECTIONS Write in the thoughts and words that show how to use the 4 STAR steps—Stop, Think, Act, Review.

We can go to my house tonight. My parents are gone for the weekend.

No one else will be there?

Stop

No!

Stop. I better think this through!

Think

Can I control myself? Is the risk worth it? Is this what is best for me? for us?

Act

I'd really like to be with you, but I don't think it's a good idea to be alone like that.

We could lose control. We're not ready for that yet.

Review

I know that was the right thing to do. We'll both be happier.

Choosing Health High School

5. Are You Ready for Sex?

A Family Discussion Activity

5 minutes, plus follow-up

MATERIALS

- Are You Ready for Sex?—Family Page (3.8)
- Are You Ready for Sex?—Student Page (3.9)
- Are You Ready for Sex?—Feedback Form (3.10)

Initiate family activity

Distribute the **Are You Ready for Sex?—Family Page, Student Page** and **Feedback Form.** Ask students to take the activity sheets home and complete this assignment with their parents or other adult family members.

Discuss family activity

Ask students to discuss the family activity in general terms. Ask students:

- In general, did you and your parent agree or disagree on the reasons teens choose to have sex?
- Did you agree or disagree on the things teens need to think about before deciding to have sex?
- Was this activity valuable? Why or why not?

Collect the **Feedback Forms** to give students credit for completing the assignment.

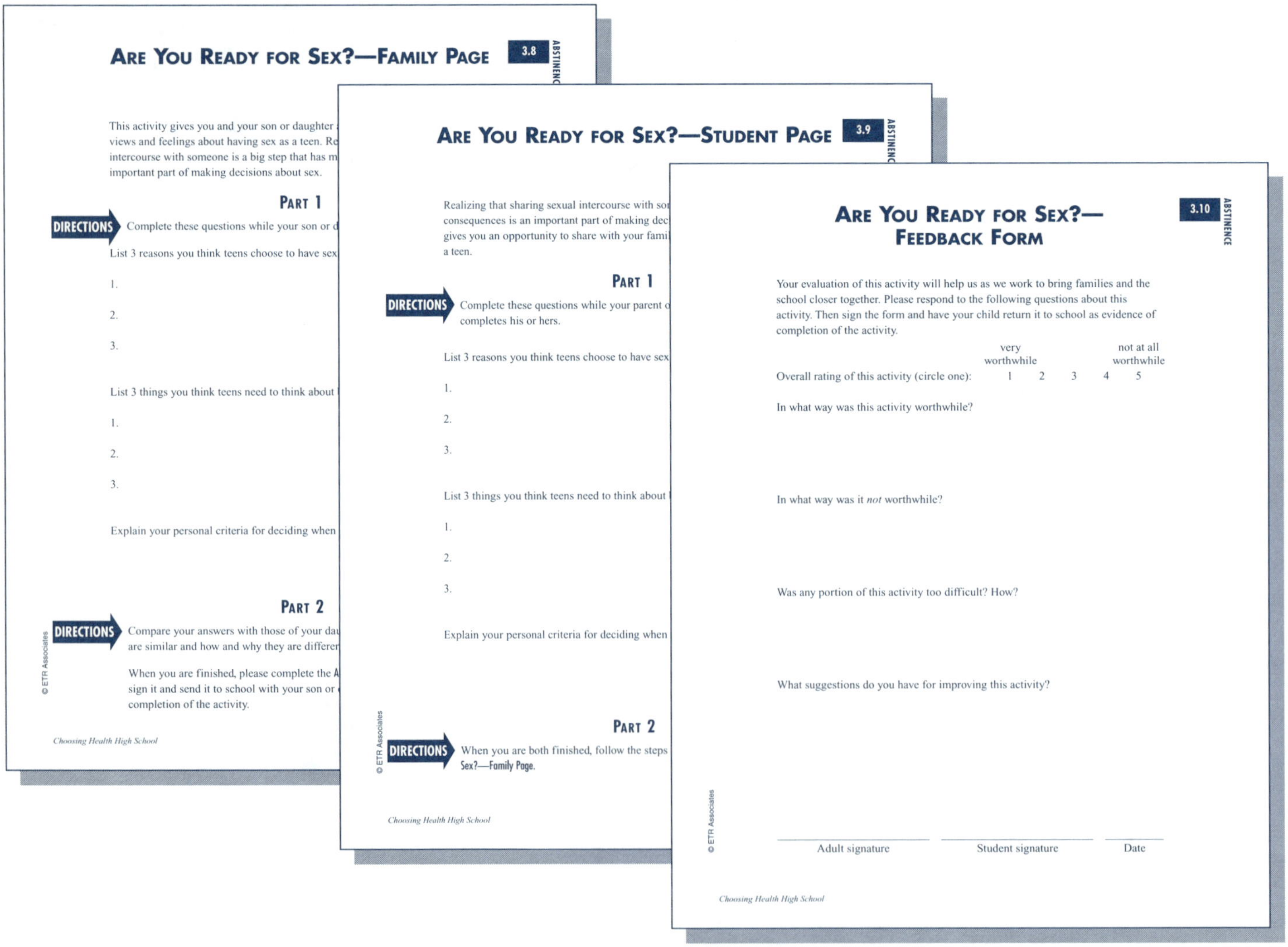

Are You Ready for Sex?—Family Page 3.8 ABSTINENCE

This activity gives you and your son or daughter ... views and feelings about having sex as a teen. R... intercourse with someone is a big step that has m... important part of making decisions about sex.

Part 1

DIRECTIONS Complete these questions while your son or d...

List 3 reasons you think teens choose to have sex...

1.

2.

3.

List 3 things you think teens need to think about ...

1.

2.

3.

Explain your personal criteria for deciding when ...

Part 2

DIRECTIONS Compare your answers with those of your da... are similar and how and why they are differe...

When you are finished, please complete the A... sign it and send it to school with your son or ... completion of the activity.

© ETR Associates

Choosing Health High School

Are You Ready for Sex?—Student Page 3.9 ABSTINENCE

Realizing that sharing sexual intercourse with so... consequences is an important part of making dec... gives you an opportunity to share with your fami... a teen.

Part 1

DIRECTIONS Complete these questions while your parent ... completes his or hers.

List 3 reasons you think teens choose to have sex...

1.

2.

3.

List 3 things you think teens need to think about ...

1.

2.

3.

Explain your personal criteria for deciding when ...

Part 2

DIRECTIONS When you are both finished, follow the steps ... **Sex?—Family Page.**

© ETR Associates

Choosing Health High School

Are You Ready for Sex?—Feedback Form 3.10 ABSTINENCE

Your evaluation of this activity will help us as we work to bring families and the school closer together. Please respond to the following questions about this activity. Then sign the form and have your child return it to school as evidence of completion of the activity.

	very worthwhile				not at all worthwhile
Overall rating of this activity (circle one):	1	2	3	4	5

In what way was this activity worthwhile?

In what way was it *not* worthwhile?

Was any portion of this activity too difficult? How?

What suggestions do you have for improving this activity?

Adult signature   Student signature   Date

© ETR Associates

Choosing Health High School

Evaluation

OBJECTIVES

Students will be able to:

1. Describe the influence of risk-taking behavior on sexual decision making.

2. Apply the decision-making process and STAR method to examples of situations of sexual temptation.

REVIEW

- Risk Taking and Self-Control *Instant Expert* (p. 50)

MATERIALS

- Evaluating Risks and Decisions (3.11)

Distribute the **Evaluating Risks and Decisions** evaluation sheet and have students complete it.

CRITERIA

Look for students to:

- correctly identify the tempting risk behavior
- state a reasonable concept of reward
- state a realistic consequence
- supply a "rule" that reflects careful decision making
- name the steps in the STAR method
- create realistic dialog that demonstrates understanding of the steps

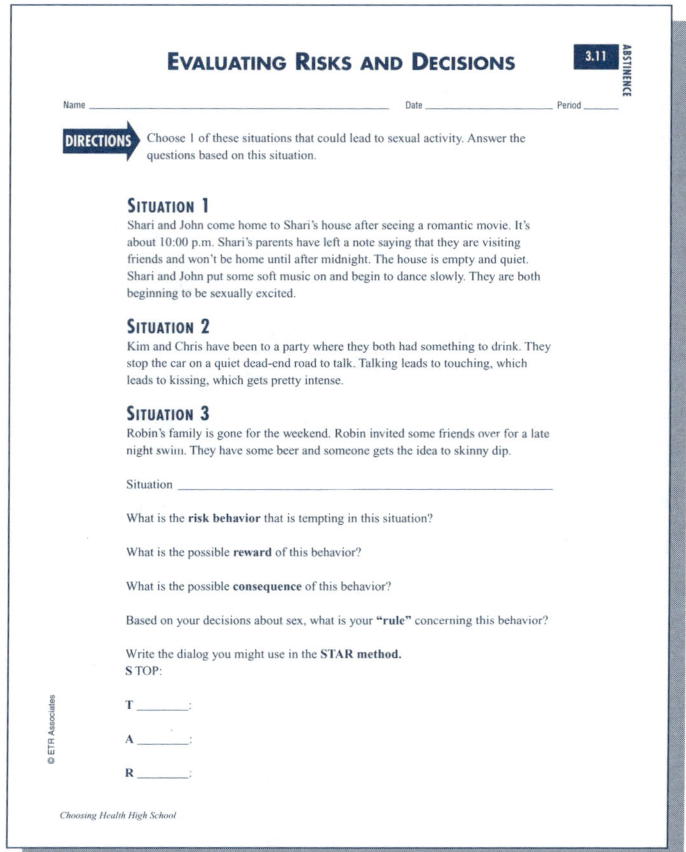

EVALUATING RISKS AND DECISIONS

3.11 ABSTINENCE

Name __________ Date __________ Period ______

DIRECTIONS Choose 1 of these situations that could lead to sexual activity. Answer the questions based on this situation.

SITUATION 1
Shari and John come home to Shari's house after seeing a romantic movie. It's about 10:00 p.m. Shari's parents have left a note saying that they are visiting friends and won't be home until after midnight. The house is empty and quiet. Shari and John put some soft music on and begin to dance slowly. They are both beginning to be sexually excited.

SITUATION 2
Kim and Chris have been to a party where they both had something to drink. They stop the car on a quiet dead-end road to talk. Talking leads to touching, which leads to kissing, which gets pretty intense.

SITUATION 3
Robin's family is gone for the weekend. Robin invited some friends over for a late night swim. They have some beer and someone gets the idea to skinny dip.

Situation __________

What is the **risk behavior** that is tempting in this situation?

What is the possible **reward** of this behavior?

What is the possible **consequence** of this behavior?

Based on your decisions about sex, what is your **"rule"** concerning this behavior?

Write the dialog you might use in the **STAR method.**
S TOP:

T ______:

A ______:

R ______:

Choosing Health High School

Risk Taking and Self-Control

Instant Expert

Risk taking can be thrilling. The thrill of a risk can undermine the self-control a person needs to be able to resist pressure, and cause him or her to act without considering the consequences. The ability to make sound decisions about what actions are best when faced with risky temptations increases a person's chances of remaining healthy and safe.

ASSESSING RISKS

Risks can have harmful consequences. Defining the real rewards of a risk, especially sexual activity, and balancing those against the possible negative consequences can help to put the risk into perspective.

Teens' perception of a risk often depends on their source of knowledge about the risk. If they have previous personal experience with a risk behavior, their assessment of the risk will be consistent with the consequences of that previous experience.

Teens may rely on information from someone else who has had experience with the risk behavior. If this source is trustworthy, it could help give them an accurate understanding of the risk. However, if their knowledge of a risk behavior comes only from its portrayal in the media (television, movies, etc.), where consequences may not be shown accurately, their ability to make decisions about the risk may be compromised.

It is important to try to develop students' understanding of the real-world rewards and consequences of various actions. Being able to weigh the rewards and the consequences of a risk helps teens determine whether the risk is worth taking.

DEVELOPING SELF-CONTROL

Humans are sexual beings and, therefore, have sexual urges. Sexual desires are natural. But we want to be able to control them and recognize the right time and place to act on them. Sexual desires are like any other desires—they carry responsibilities with them. If a person has the desire to drive a car, he or she must have a license and agree to follow the rules of the road.

Similarly, teens need to identify what their own rules around sexual behavior are. Understanding the balance of risk—the rewards and consequences of an action—and looking clearly at personal values will help an individual determine these rules. Rules come from consideration of what is right and acceptable within one's own value system. Once a person has decided what rules feel right, he or she must be able to act on those decisions.

(continued...)

Risk Taking and Self-Control

Instant Expert

Self-control is the ability to follow the rules we set for ourselves. It is strengthened by understanding the possible consequences of an action and enables a person to stop to think about these consequences *before* acting. Students may not be ready to deal with the consequences of being sexually active. Yet the temptations all around them to become sexually involved can lead to impulsive actions with damaging results. Being able to use self-control in a tempting situation increases students' chances of acting responsibly and following the rules they have set for themselves.

DECISION MAKING

Decision making is key to following the rules we choose for ourselves. In some risk situations, there is time to make appropriate decisions. Sexual situations often offer little time for deliberation. Sexual drives and the sexual response cycle can sometimes compromise a person's ability to think clearly, particularly if emotional needs are also strong.

Therefore, it is extremely important for students to consider what actions are acceptable to them *before* they find themselves in a tempting situation. A 5-step decision-making model provides students with the opportunity to consider their personal rules for sexual activity. The steps include:

1. Gather **information.**
2. List possible **solutions.**
3. List **consequences** of each solution.
4. **Choose** the best solution and try it.
5. **Evaluate** the outcome.

(continued...)

Risk Taking and Self-Control

Instant Expert

THE STAR METHOD

Once personal rules have been established, it is important to have the skills to use them. The STAR method is an easy way for students to apply the rules. STAR stands for Stop, Think, Act, Review.

Stop: First students will *stop* by mentally telling themselves, "Wait, I need to think this through."

Think: This step gives them time to consider the consequences of certain actions and the rules they have established for themselves. Questions such as the following can help students *think:*

- Is it really worth it?
- How will I feel after doing this?
- Could I or anyone else be harmed by this action?
- What is the most honest, ethical thing to do?
- Does this fit with the rules I've made for myself?

Act: After careful consideration, students *act* on the decision. This is their cue to do what they think is best.

Review: This step encourages students to evaluate the results of their decision and add this experience to their knowledge for future use.

Understanding and practicing the STAR method allows students to reinforce the self-control skills that can help them act responsibly, not impulsively.

Decisions about sexual activity are very important in students' lives. These decisions can make a major difference to their futures and current happiness. The best decisions are made *before* students find themselves in the middle of a situation in which thinking clearly is difficult. Applying the personal rules they have established around sexual behaviors and making a decision to follow these rules is easier if students use the STAR method.

UNIT

4

No in Words and Actions

TIME

3–4 periods

ACTIVITIES

1. A Good Listener
2. Clear Communication
3. Being Assertive in Saying No
4. Delaying and Refusing Skills
5. Practicing the Skills
6. Saying No

UNIT

4

NO IN WORDS AND ACTIONS

OBJECTIVES

Students will be able to:

1. Demonstrate the use of listening skills and I-statements.
2. Demonstrate the use of assertive communication.
3. Demonstrate the use of delay and refusal skills.

GETTING STARTED

Have:

- markers
- box
- posterboard or butcher paper, 6 pieces

Make transparency of:

- Listening: An Important Skill (4.1)
- "I" and "You" Statements (4.2)
- Assertiveness (4.4)
- Refusal Steps (4.5)
- The Story of Jamie and Lee (4.6)
- Saying No in Words and Actions (4.12)

Copy 1 for each student:

- How Would You Respond? (4.3)
- Jamie and Lee (4.7)
- Cartoon Dialog (4.8)
- Saying No—Family and Student Page (4.10)
- Saying No—Feedback Form (4.11)

Copy:

- Delays and Refusals Cards (4.9), 4–6 copies

SPECIAL STEPS

Prepare a set of Delays and Refusals Cards and label pieces of posterboard. See Activity 5 (p. 65).

Unit Overview

PURPOSE

Students have studied the pressures they face to be sexually active and have practiced making decisions that are healthful. The ability to say no, both in words and actions, will enable students to follow through on the decisions they have made for themselves concerning sexual abstinence. Increasing students' skills in communicating clearly, being assertive and refusing in ways that maintain relationships will increase the probability that they will remain abstinent.

MAIN POINTS

* Using good listening skills and I-statements increases the clarity of communication, especially when saying no.
* Assertiveness skills increase one's ability to say no effectively.
* Delay and refusal skills help teens say no yet still feel accepted and maintain relationships.

REVIEW

To increase your understanding of delay and refusal skills, review **No in Words and Actions** ***Instant Expert*** (p. 70).

VOCABULARY

aggressive—Hostile, demanding, pushy, demeaning of others.

assertiveness—Standing up for what one believes, wants or needs without denying the rights of others.

delay—To put off to a later time.

delaying tactics—Techniques that give a person time to decide what to do or how to refuse.

I-statement—A way to express thoughts, feelings and needs while respecting the rights of others.

passive—Submissive, inactive, yielding to others.

refusal skills—Methods of declining to do something.

you-statement—Message that blames others for actions and results.

1. A Good Listener

A Dyad Discussion Activity

15 minutes

MATERIALS

- transparency of Listening: An Important Skill (4.1)

✷

Students practice listening

Ask students to choose a partner, preferably someone they do not know well. Explain the assignment:

- Take turns telling each other about yourself for 30 seconds.
- The listening partner may not respond in any way—no questions, signals or facial expressions.
- When the first 30 seconds are up, the second partner will have 30 seconds to talk about herself or himself.

When students understand the assignment, begin timing and have the first partners begin speaking. At the end of 30 seconds, have the partners switch roles and time students for another 30 seconds.

(continued...)

Listening: An Important Skill 4.1 ABSTINENCE

Good Listening

- Facing the speaker.
- Making eye contact.
- Paying close attention.
- Giving nonverbal feedback to show you are listening, e.g., nod head.
- Asking questions to clarify as needed.
- Trying to understand the feelings of the speaker.
- Not allowing your personal views to affect your understanding.

Poor Listening

- Sitting facing away from the speaker.
- Looking around the room, not at the speaker.
- Body language that says you are not interested.
- Doing something else while trying to listen.
- Interrupting in the middle of an idea.
- Making unrelated remarks.
- Changing the subject before the speaker is finished.
- Talking to someone else while the speaker is talking.
- Trying to top the speaker's story with one of your own.
- Thinking about how you will respond before you hear all the speaker has to say.
- Putting the speaker down because you don't agree.

Choosing Health High School

1. A Good Listener

Continued

Recap activity

Ask for a few volunteers to report to the class what they heard from their partners. Ask students:

- Was this task easy for the speaker?
- What was difficult for the first speaker? the second speaker?
- What was difficult for the listener?

Discuss listening skills

Ask students what they think a good listener should do. Display the **Listening: An Important Skill** transparency and discuss the listed skills. Explain that listening is an important communication skill.

SHARPEN THE SKILL

COMMUNICATION—OBSERVING LISTENING SKILLS

Have students look for the points on the **Listening: An Important Skill** transparency as they observe people in social situations. Ask them to report on their observations in general terms. (The people observed should remain anonymous.)

2. Clear Communication

A Roleplay Activity

25 minutes

MATERIALS

- transparency of "I" and "You" Statements (4.2)
- How Would You Respond? (4.3)

✷

MEETING STUDENT NEEDS

Some students work best when they have the opportunity to work verbally and others work best in written form. You may want to complete the **How Would You Respond?** activity sheet by having students work with a partner and respond verbally.

Discuss scenario

Read this scenario to the class: Your little sister or brother read your journal and then told your mom a very private secret.

Ask for a student to pretend to be the little sister or brother. Then ask a few volunteers to respond to the little sister or brother as if they had just found out what she or he had done.

After the volunteers have shared, ask them:

- What *behavior* did you respond to? (reading journal and telling mom a secret)
- What was the *effect* of this behavior? (privacy violated, mom may have questioned you about it, can't trust your sibling))
- How did you *feel* as a result? (angry, hurt, embarrassed, distrustful, vengeful)

(continued...)

"I" and "You" Statements

4.2 ABSTINENCE

You-statement: "You are so irresponsible. You are always late and now you're making me late!"

I-statement: "I depend on you to pick me up on time to get to practice. If I'm late, I get in trouble. I feel angry because I was ready on time."

The Parts of an I-Statement

1. **Behavior:** Name the behavior.
   Example: "I depend on you to pick me up on time to get to practice."
2. **Effect:** Explain how the behavior affects you.
   Example: "If I'm late I get in trouble."
3. **Feeling:** Explain how you feel.
   Example: "I feel angry because I was ready on time."

Practice for I-Statements

- Your friend takes you out to lunch and eats so slowly that you are late for math class.
  Example: Lunch took so long that I was late for math class and had to go to detention. I felt embarrassed.
- Your good friend is angry with Terry, who is also a friend of yours. Your friend often starts saying critical things about Terry to you.
  Example: I understand that you are angry with Terry and want to talk about it, but Terry is also a friend of mine. I feel uncomfortable because I feel caught in the middle between you and Terry.
- You practiced and know your lines for the play, but the person you have a scene with still doesn't know her lines.
  Example: I've noticed you have to look at the script a lot during rehearsal. It's hard for me to do our scene when you don't know the lines. I feel frustrated because I want our scene to go well.

Choosing Health High School

2. Clear Communication

Continued

Discuss I-statements

Explain that 3 components—behavior, effect and feeling—make up an I-statement. An I-statement is a way to express feelings, thoughts and needs clearly, while respecting the other person. I-statements are a way to help communication.

Display the **"I" and "You" Statements** transparency, keeping the practice situations covered. Review the example of each type of message. Discuss the difference between I-statements and you-statements, using the **No in Words and Actions *Instant Expert*** as a guide. Ask students to comment on how they would feel if someone said the you-statement versus the I-statement.

Review the 3 parts of an I-statement listed on the transparency. Then reveal the practice situations one at a time, keeping the example I-statement covered. Ask students to identify the behavior in each practice situation. For each situation, ask for a volunteer who can phrase an I-statement. Identify all 3 components in the response. Then share the example on the transparency, again pointing out the 3 components.

(continued...)

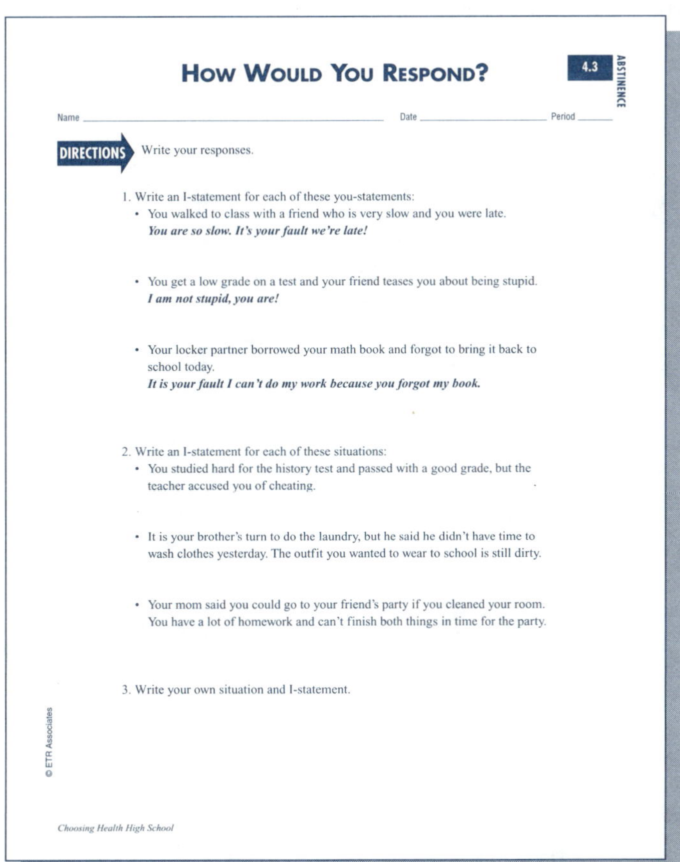

How Would You Respond?

4.3 ABSTINENCE

Name ______________________ Date ____________ Period ______

DIRECTIONS Write your responses.

1. Write an I-statement for each of these you-statements:
   - You walked to class with a friend who is very slow and you were late.
     You are so slow. It's your fault we're late!
   - You get a low grade on a test and your friend teases you about being stupid.
     I am not stupid, you are!
   - Your locker partner borrowed your math book and forgot to bring it back to school today.
     It is your fault I can't do my work because you forgot my book.
2. Write an I-statement for each of these situations:
   - You studied hard for the history test and passed with a good grade, but the teacher accused you of cheating.
   - It is your brother's turn to do the laundry, but he said he didn't have time to wash clothes yesterday. The outfit you wanted to wear to school is still dirty.
   - Your mom said you could go to your friend's party if you cleaned your room. You have a lot of homework and can't finish both things in time for the party.
3. Write your own situation and I-statement.

Choosing Health High School

EXTEND THE LEARNING

Ask students to keep an I-Statement Journal for the next 3 days. In this journal, they will record at least 2 things that happened each day (the behavior), the *effect* of the behavior and how they *felt* about it. Example: Today I did all of my homework right after school (behavior) so that I was able to watch both of my favorite TV shows (effect), which really made me feel good about myself (feeling). Discuss the results.

2. Clear Communication

Continued

MEETING STUDENT NEEDS

Provide each group with a set of table tents (small folded papers) identifying the role they have in the group practice activity—speaker, active listener, observer—to help students focus and stay on task. It will also assist you in observing the groups.

Students write I-statements

Distribute the **How Would You Respond?** activity sheet and ask students to respond to the situation with an I-statement. Have them work individually and write their responses on the activity sheet.

Groups roleplay I-statements

Divide the class into groups of 3 to roleplay their responses and practice active listening. Explain the group assignment:

- One person will read his or her responses on the **How Would You Respond?** activity sheet.
- The second person will listen actively.
- The third person will observe the first 2 and comment on how well they listened and used the 3 components of an I-statement.
- Then exchange roles with each other until all 3 partners have had all 3 roles.

Ongoing Assessment Observe student roleplays to see evidence of active listening skills as well as use of the components of I-statements. Collect the activity sheets and review students' responses. See the **No in Words and Actions** ***Instant Expert*** for assessment criteria.

3. Being Assertive in Saying No

A Class Discussion Activity

Define assertiveness

Ask students to share ideas on the definition of assertiveness. Lead students to develop a definition such as the following:

Assertiveness is the ability to say what you think and stand up for what you believe in without violating the rights of others. Being assertive shows that you are in control of yourself and the situation.

Compare assertive, aggressive and passive responses

Discuss the differences between assertive, aggressive and passive behavior, using the **No in Words and Actions** ***Instant Expert*** as a guide.

Share this example: In a restaurant you order a hamburger and fries. The waiter brings you a cheeseburger and fries. You hate cheese. Your response:

- **Passive:** You say nothing. You try to scrape off the cheese and eat the burger.
- **Aggressive:** "How stupid are you? I ordered a hamburger. I hate cheese! Bring me a hamburger right now!"
- **Assertive:** "I ordered a hamburger and you brought me a cheeseburger. I really don't like cheese. Could you please bring me a hamburger?"

Ask students how they would feel if they were the waiter in each of these situations.

Discuss assertive responses

Display the **Assertiveness** transparency and review the 3 steps. Ask for volunteers to give responses to the practice situations. Ask 1 volunteer to demonstrate a passive response, a second to demonstrate an aggressive response, and a third to demonstrate an assertive response. Carefully monitor the assertive responses for use of all 3 steps.

Discuss the difference in how people would feel and what might happen after each type of response.

Discuss nonverbal communication

Discuss the importance of nonverbal communication: tone of voice and body language (posture). Ask volunteers to restate some of the assertive statements just given using a tone of voice and body posture that back up the statement.

(continued...)

40 minutes

✱

MATERIALS

- transparency of Assertiveness (4.4)

MEETING STUDENT NEEDS

During the oral practice, have small signs available that say "passive," "aggressive" and "assertive." Ask each volunteer to hold up the sign for the type of response he or she is demonstrating. This will clarify each response and help your visual learners identify each type.

CONTINUED

SHARPEN THE SKILL
ASSERTIVENESS—PARTNER EXCHANGE

Offer additional practice with a "free exchange practice." Each student holds up his or her hand when ready to work with a partner. Students join with others who are ready to practice. They continue to find new partners to practice with by signaling in this way.

EXTEND THE LEARNING

If students have been keeping an I-Statement Journal, they can add daily entries on assertiveness. Ask them to include information about the situation, what was said and what could have been said that would have been more assertive.

Students practice assertiveness

Ask students to write 2 assertive statements of their own in response to 2 of the practice ideas on the **Assertiveness** transparency. Have them find a partner to share these statements with. Ask partners to respond by providing feedback on whether both the verbal and nonverbal messages were clear. If students need more practice, have them trade partners and continue practicing.

Ongoing Assessment Observe students during class discussions and practice sessions to assess their ability to demonstrate assertive responses that reflect the 3 components:

- stating a position
- offering a reason
- recognizing how others will feel

ASSERTIVENESS 4.4 ABSTINENCE

3 Steps

1. **State your *position*.** Say exactly what you mean:
   - "No, I don't want to do that."
   - "I would rather…"
   - "I believe that is…"
2. **Offer a *reason*.** Sometimes you may want to help others understand you better by explaining why:
   - "…because…"
3. **Recognize the other person's *feelings*.** Choose your words carefully to show you understand how others feel:
   - "…I imagine you feel…"
   - "…I can see how you'd feel…"

Practice for Assertiveness

1. You are standing in line to buy concert tickets and someone cuts in front of you.
2. Your brother or sister has borrowed your favorite sweater without permission.
3. Your friends want to go to an R-rated movie and you don't want to go.
4. Your parents are gone for the weekend so your boyfriend or girlfriend suggests spending the evening at your house.
5. Your boyfriend or girlfriend keeps trying to touch you too intimately.
6. Your boyfriend or girlfriend tells you that having sex will make you a real man or woman.
7. Your boyfriend or girlfriend says that if you were really in love you'd have sex together.
8. Your boyfriend or girlfriend tells you that it's OK to have sex because he or she will take care of everything.

Choosing Health High School

4. Delaying and Refusing Skills

A Class Discussion Activity

Discuss the importance of saying no

Explain that once students have made healthful decisions, they will need the skills to follow through and be able to say no. Acknowledge that many of us need help to overcome the pressure we face to stick with our decisions.

Discuss delaying tactics

Explain that *delaying tactics* offer a way to put off responding until you can figure out how best to respond. A delaying tactic is simply a way of saying that you will have to think more about it.

Read this scenario to the class and ask each student to respond with a delaying statement:

> You and your girlfriend/boyfriend are leaving a movie on Friday night. She/he says, "I think we should go to my house. No one else will be there for 5 hours." You don't really think it is a good idea to be alone together but you want more time to think about how to say no. You could delay by saying ______.

(continued...)

Refusal Steps

4.5 ABSTINENCE

1. **Ask questions.** Clarify what friends are asking you to do:
   - "Exactly what are you suggesting?"
   - "What would we do?"
2. **Name the trouble.** Say why you think this is a problem:
   - "There are too many risks for us now."
   - "That breaks the rules we made for ourselves."
3. **Identify the consequences.** Say what you think might happen if you do this:
   - "I/you could get pregnant."
   - "The risk of getting an STD is just too great."
   - "Our relationship is just not ready for this step yet. We could end up feeling really guilty and breaking up."
4. **Suggest alternatives.** Name other things you could do together:
   - "Instead of being alone, why don't we go to the movies?"
   - "Instead of being alone, why don't we go over to Julie's house?"
5. **Move on.** Walk away as you offer an alternative:
   - "If you change your mind, I'll be at Julie's. We can still go to the movie."

Refusing Under Pressure

If someone really pressures you:

- **Stop.** Look at the person directly and tell him or her to listen to you.
- **Stay calm.** Repeat what you said about the problem, consequences and alternatives.
- **Walk away.** Get away from the person and the situation.

Choosing Health High School

MATERIALS

- transparency of Refusal Steps (4.5)
- transparency of The Story of Jamie and Lee (4.6)
- Jamie and Lee (4.7)

4. Delaying and Refusing Skills

CONTINUED

> **MEETING STUDENT NEEDS**
>
> The names in this sample story are gender neutral to allow all students to feel comfortable responding. Encourage both males and females to respond to all of the statements in this oral exercise.
>
> 

Discuss refusals

Display the **Refusal Steps** transparency. Explain that these steps will help students say no in ways that will still maintain the relationship with the other person. Discuss each step with students, using the **No in Words and Actions *Instant Expert*** as a guide. Give an example of each step as you discuss it.

Create refusal dialog

Display **The Story of Jamie and Lee** transparency and distribute the **Jamie and Lee** activity sheet. Read the story from the transparency and ask students to fill in the dialog for each step in refusing on the activity sheet. Suggest what might be said in response to each refusal statement and continue to the next step. You might choose to read the story a second or third time, asking for different responses for each step.

The Story of Jamie and Lee

4.6 ABSTINENCE

Jamie and Lee have been going out for 3 months. They are both seniors, looking forward to graduating from high school in 5 months. This is the first time either one has had a serious relationship. They are very happy together.

Together they made a decision to be abstinent because of all the possible negative consequences from being sexually intimate—the possibility of pregnancy or STD, guilt from going against their beliefs, stress on their relationship, etc. But lately it has been harder and harder to keep that decision.

They have just come from the homecoming dance. They get to Lee's house and find no one is home. Jamie suggests they sit together on the couch to talk. Lee isn't sure where that might lead.

Choosing Health High School

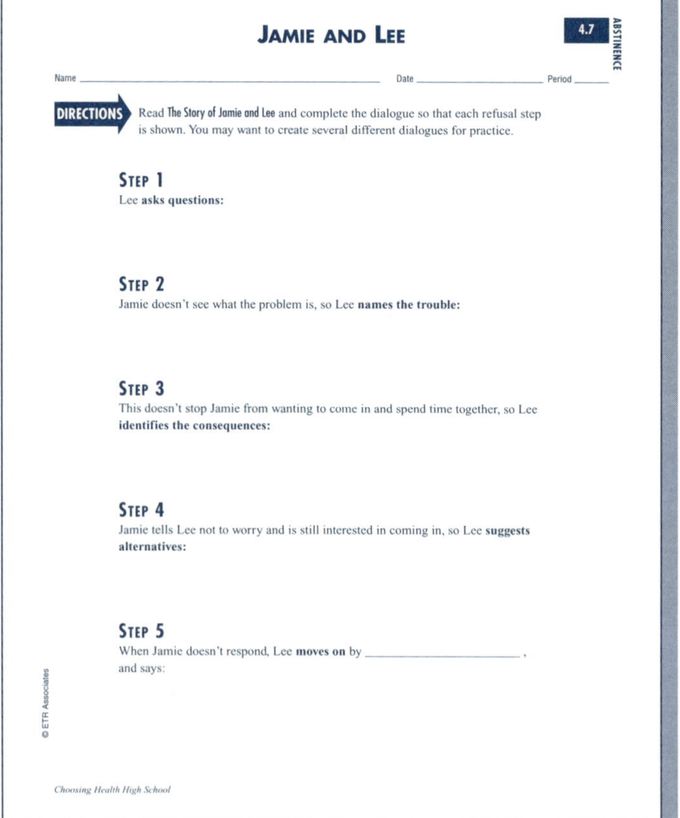

Jamie and Lee

4.7 ABSTINENCE

Name ______________________ Date ______________ Period ______

DIRECTIONS Read **The Story of Jamie and Lee** and complete the dialogue so that each refusal step is shown. You may want to create several different dialogues for practice.

Step 1
Lee **asks questions:**

Step 2
Jamie doesn't see what the problem is, so Lee **names the trouble:**

Step 3
This doesn't stop Jamie from wanting to come in and spend time together, so Lee **identifies the consequences:**

Step 4
Jamie tells Lee not to worry and is still interested in coming in, so Lee **suggests alternatives:**

Step 5
When Jamie doesn't respond, Lee **moves on** by ______________________,
and says:

Choosing Health High School

5. Practicing the Skills

A Small Group Activity

Students create cartoons

Distribute the **Cartoon Dialog** activity sheet and ask students to create a cartoon that demonstrates the refusal process. Ask them to include the following elements:

- Name and describe the 2 characters.
- Describe the type of relationship they have.
- Detail the situation for this scene.
- Write the dialog between the characters, showing the steps in the refusal process. Include a delaying statement.
- Underline each of the refusal and delaying statements in your dialog.

Students share cartoons

As students complete the **Cartoon Dialog** activity sheet, move around the classroom with the box of **Delays and Refusals Cards.** Have each student draw a card from the box.

When students have completed their dialogs, ask for volunteers to read them to the class. Ask the other students to listen carefully as the dialogs are read. Have them keep a list of any statements in the dialogs that represent the refusal step listed on the card they drew.

Groups create posters

Divide the class into 6 small groups according to the **Delays and Refusals Cards** they drew—Delay, Ask Questions, Name the Trouble, Identify the Consequences, Suggest Alternatives, Move On. Give each group a piece of posterboard or butcher paper labeled with the name of their step. Explain the group assignment:

- Combine your lists of statements from the dialogs.
- Write the statements that represent your refusal step on the poster.
- Add any other statements that would be useful examples of your step.

(continued...)

DELAYS AND REFUSALS CARDS

Make enough copies of the **Delays and Refusals Cards (4.9)** teacher page to create a card for each student. Try to have an equal number of cards for each step. Place the cards in a box or other container so students can draw a card without looking.

Take 6 pieces of posterboard or butcher paper and label each with a different refusal step.

35 minutes

MATERIALS

- ♦ Cartoon Dialog (4.8)
- prepared Delays and Refusals Cards
- box
- labeled posterboards
- markers

MEETING STUDENT NEEDS

Students with limited writing skills might be more successful working with a partner in developing the cartoon dialog. You might give students the option of working alone or with a partner and guide students to choose partners who complement their own skills.

5. Practicing the Skills

Continued

Sharpen the Skill

Assertiveness—Teaching Others

Have students develop a lesson plan to teach the steps for effective refusals to elementary school students. Work with an elementary teacher to arrange a visit to an upper elementary class to teach the skills using high school peers.

Groups report

Ask groups to share their posters with the class. Discuss each step of the refusal process again, reminding students that these statements can help them say no while allowing them to maintain their friendships.

Display the posters in the classroom, with the steps in order.

Ongoing Assessment Review the **Cartoon Dialog** activity sheet to see that students have included a delaying statement and accurately represented each of the 5 steps:

- Ask questions.
- Name the trouble.
- Identify the consequences.
- Suggest alternatives.
- Move on.

Review group posters for creativity and accuracy.

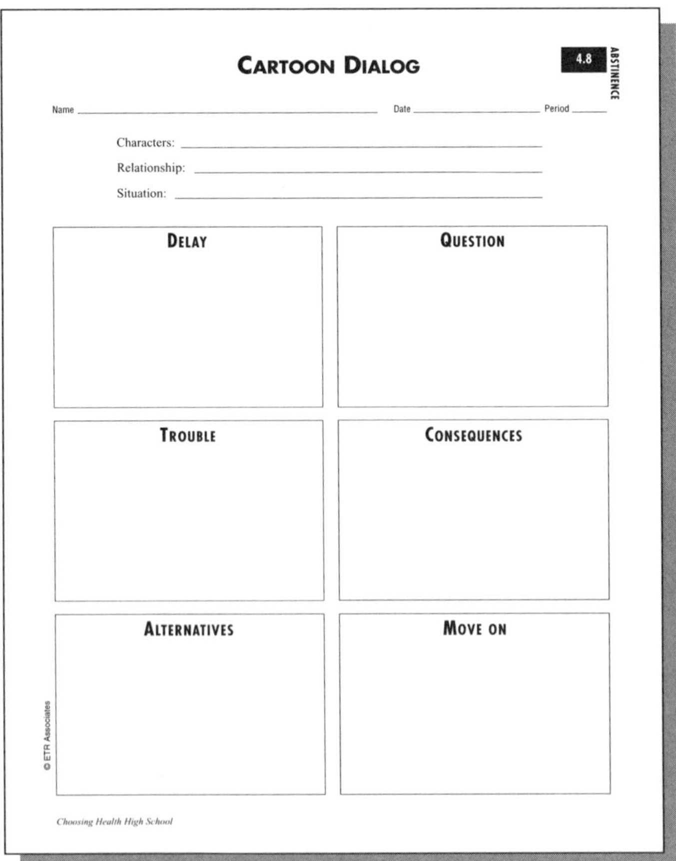

Cartoon Dialog

4.8 Abstinence

Name ______ Date ______ Period ______

Characters: ______

Relationship: ______

Situation: ______

Delay	Question
Trouble	Consequences
Alternatives	Move On

© ETR Associates

Choosing Health High School

6. Saying No

A Family Discussion Activity

MATERIALS

- Saying No—Family and Student Page (4.10)
- Saying No—Feedback Form (4.11)

Initiate family activity

Distribute the **Saying No—Family and Student Page** and **Feedback Form.** Ask students to take the activity sheets home and complete this assignment with their parents or other adult family members.

Discuss family activity

Ask students to discuss the family activity in general terms. Ask students:

- Do you think these skills would be effective in a real-life situation? Why or why not?
- Did you and your adult family member switch roles? If so, how did it feel to receive a refusal that used the skills?
- Was this opportunity to practice the refusal skills useful to you? Why or why not?

Collect the **Feedback Forms** to give students credit for completing the assignment.

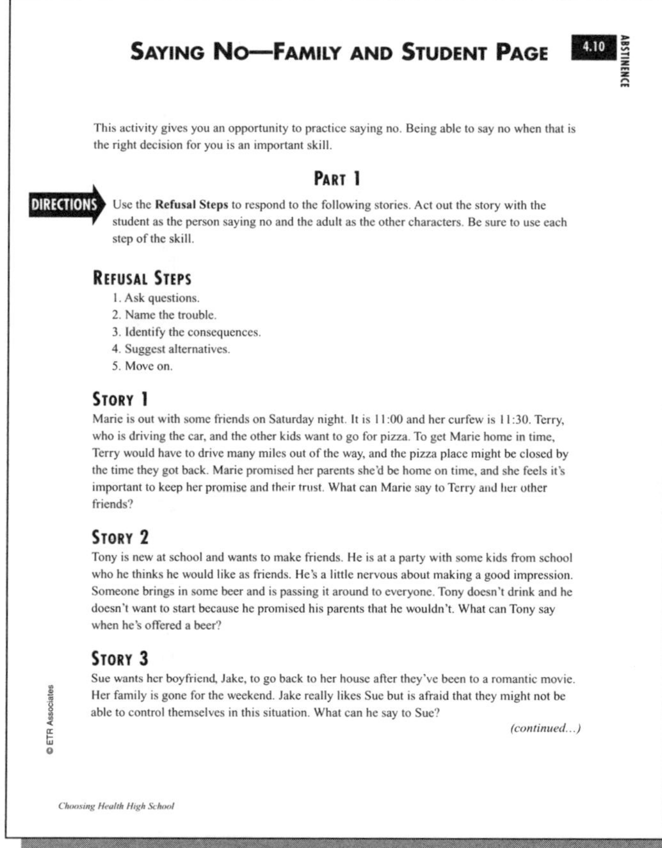

Saying No—Family and Student Page 4.10 ABSTINENCE

This activity gives you an opportunity to practice saying no. Being able to say no when that is the right decision for you is an important skill.

Part 1

DIRECTIONS Use the **Refusal Steps** to respond to the following stories. Act out the story with the student as the person saying no and the adult as the other characters. Be sure to use each step of the skill.

Refusal Steps

1. Ask questions.
2. Name the trouble.
3. Identify the consequences.
4. Suggest alternatives.
5. Move on.

Story 1

Marie is out with some friends on Saturday night. It is 11:00 and her curfew is 11:30. Terry, who is driving the car, and the other kids want to go for pizza. To get Marie home in time, Terry would have to drive many miles out of the way, and the pizza place might be closed by the time they got back. Marie promised her parents she'd be home on time, and she feels it's important to keep her promise and their trust. What can Marie say to Terry and her other friends?

Story 2

Tony is new at school and wants to make friends. He is at a party with some kids from school who he thinks he would like as friends. He's a little nervous about making a good impression. Someone brings in some beer and is passing it around to everyone. Tony doesn't drink and he doesn't want to start because he promised his parents that he wouldn't. What can Tony say when he's offered a beer?

Story 3

Sue wants her boyfriend, Jake, to go back to her house after they've been to a romantic movie. Her family is gone for the weekend. Jake really likes Sue but is afraid that they might not be able to control themselves in this situation. What can he say to Sue?

(continued...)

Choosing Health High School

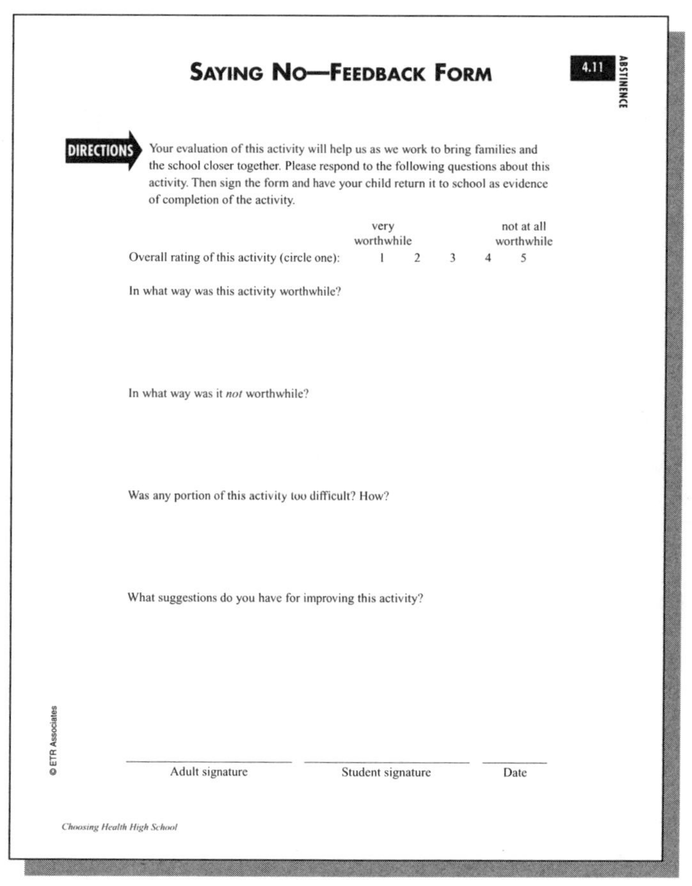

Saying No—Feedback Form 4.11 ABSTINENCE

DIRECTIONS Your evaluation of this activity will help us as we work to bring families and the school closer together. Please respond to the following questions about this activity. Then sign the form and have your child return it to school as evidence of completion of the activity.

	very worthwhile				not at all worthwhile
Overall rating of this activity (circle one):	1	2	3	4	5

In what way was this activity worthwhile?

In what way was it *not* worthwhile?

Was any portion of this activity too difficult? How?

What suggestions do you have for improving this activity?

Adult signature ________ Student signature ________ Date ________

Choosing Health High School

Evaluation

20 minutes

REVIEW

- No in Words and Actions *Instant Expert* (p. 70)

MATERIALS

- Saying No in Words and Actions (4.12)

✸

OBJECTIVE

Students will be able to:

1. Demonstrate the use of listening skills and I-statements.

2. Demonstrate the use of assertive communication.

3. Demonstrate the use of delay and refusal skills.

Distribute the **Saying No in Words and Actions** evaluation sheet. Review the directions and solicit ideas from the class for a situation to use. As a class, create the first line of dialog. Then allow students to complete the roleplay dialog on their own.

(continued...)

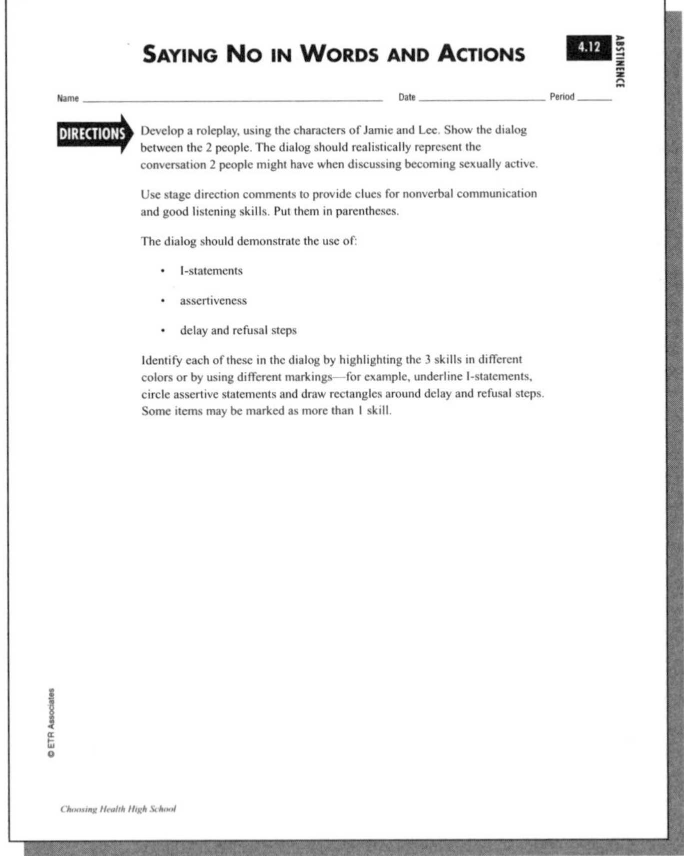

Saying No in Words and Actions 4.12 ABSTINENCE

Name ______ Date ______ Period ______

DIRECTIONS Develop a roleplay, using the characters of Jamie and Lee. Show the dialog between the 2 people. The dialog should realistically represent the conversation 2 people might have when discussing becoming sexually active.

Use stage direction comments to provide clues for nonverbal communication and good listening skills. Put them in parentheses.

The dialog should demonstrate the use of:

- I-statements
- assertiveness
- delay and refusal steps

Identify each of these in the dialog by highlighting the 3 skills in different colors or by using different markings—for example, underline I-statements, circle assertive statements and draw rectangles around delay and refusal steps. Some items may be marked as more than 1 skill.

© ETR Associates

Choosing Health High School

EVALUATION

CONTINUED

CRITERIA

Evaluate students' responses for the following elements:

- the use and correct identification of I-statements, assertive communication, and delay and refusal steps
- the number of times I-statements and assertive statements are used
- the use of all refusal steps in order
- the creativity and real-world flow of the dialog

MEETING STUDENT NEEDS

The kinesthetic learners in the class will benefit by being able to present their roleplays as dramatic skits or using some type of puppets as the characters. These could be paper cutouts, paper bag characters, hand puppets, etc. They could make these as part of the activity or you could have a collection available.

Another way to assist these learners is to provide some basic costume items, such as hats, scarves, jackets, etc., that could help create the mood.

No in Words and Actions

Instant Expert

Once students make decisions about what they want to do and what they expect from themselves, they must learn how to follow through on those decisions in their daily lives. Decisions teens make about sexual abstinence may often be challenged. The ability to say no is extremely important in carrying out a decision to be abstinent. Learning certain skills can make saying no easier and more effective.

COMMUNICATION SKILLS

Clear communication is an important element of the ability to say no. When opportunities to be sexually active arise, clear communication is the first step in assessing and understanding the desires and intentions involved. Communication skills include:

- active listening
- I-statements
- nonverbal signals

Active Listening

Active listening increases the opportunity for people to understand each other and feel valued, as well as ensures that the messages sent are those that are received. Good listening skills can be practiced every day. This practice will help increase effectiveness when more serious issues arise.

I-Statements

I-statements allow people to take responsibility for their thoughts and feelings without accusing other people or denying others' rights. I-statements are statements that reflect a person's feelings about a behavior and its results. Clear communication with I-statements helps people be more assertive and able to say no when they want to.

The opposite of an I-statement is a you-statement, which blames others for the behavior and result, rather than expressing one's own feelings. People often feel attacked by a you-statement but feel understood if an I-statements is used in the same situation. An I-statement expresses a person's own feelings about what happened, without blaming the other person.

I-statements have 3 important parts:

- naming the behavior
- describing the effect of the behavior
- stating what feeling arose in the speaker as a result

(continued...)

No in Words and Actions

Instant Expert

The following is an example of an I-statement: "When you have the TV on loudly when I'm doing my homework, it's hard for me to concentrate. Then I feel frustrated." Using I-statements takes practice but is essential to clear communication.

Nonverbal Signals

Nonverbal signals are used to back up verbal messages. Listeners are very confused when they receive conflicting messages—words that say no, but actions that say yes.

Nonverbal signals include facial expressions, body language, tone of voice and gestures. Examples of confusing nonverbal signals are nodding the head up and down but verbally saying no, or saying yes with a questioning look.

PASSIVE, AGGRESSIVE OR ASSERTIVE?

Once the skills for clear communication are developed, students need to be able to function assertively rather than aggressively or passively. Assertiveness means standing up for one's own rights, thoughts and beliefs in a manner that does not infringe on the rights of others.

Aggressiveness is defending one's own rights by infringing on the rights of others. Aggressive responses might be hostile, demanding or pushy. Aggressive words or actions often demean or show disrespect for someone else, which can lead to confrontation.

Passiveness means giving up one's own rights in deference to those of others. Responding passively means a person holds back ideas, opinions and feelings. This can be hurtful to all parties involved and result in misunderstandings.

3 Steps to Assertiveness

The skill of being assertive can be broken down into 3 steps:

- stating a position
- offering a reason for it
- recognizing how others will feel

An assertive statement makes a person's position clear, while being considerate of the other person. This type of statement allows a message to be received without hostility and usually leads to a discussion rather than an argument. An example of an assertive statement is, "No, I don't want to have sex now, because I don't think our relationship is ready for that step. I know you are probably disappointed."

(continued...)

No in Words and Actions

Instant Expert

DELAYS AND REFUSALS

There are many pressures on teens today to be sexually active. Being clear, assertive communicators will help them to say no. However, they may sometimes deal with partners who do not have good communication skills and may continue to apply pressure to have sex. When this happens, the use of delay and refusal skills becomes very important.

Delaying Tactics

Sometimes people need more time to think about something. Sometimes they know they want to say no but just can't seem to do it at the time. A delaying statement is quite simple: it says that a person wants more time to respond; for example, "I need to think about it for a while."

Delaying tactics are used to "buy time." They enable a person to avoid the issue or postpone dealing with it for a while. The issue is likely to arise again, however, at which time a clear refusal will be needed.

The Refusal Process

The simplest refusal is indeed to "just say no." But often just saying no is difficult in a relationship where sexual activity has been suggested. The pressure to be sexually active that comes from peers, society and teens' own physical urges can be very strong. Delaying tactics will only work up to a point. Eventually skills for effective refusals are needed.

A good refusal process allows a person to say no in a way that maintains the relationship. Teens need to believe they can say no without losing their friends. The fear of feeling alienated and friendless is often the reason teens fail to say no.

The following 5-step refusal process is designed to build communication between people so that the no answer makes more sense and does not jeopardize the relationship.

1. Ask questions.
2. Name the trouble.
3. Identify the consequences.
4. Suggest alternatives.
5. Move on.

(continued...)

No in Words and Actions

Instant Expert

1. **Ask questions.** Asking questions allows a person to clarify what is being proposed. Sometimes the assumptions we make about what a person means are not really accurate. Asking questions reduces the chances of misunderstanding.
2. **Name the trouble.** Naming the trouble with the proposed activity puts it into perspective. The trouble might be that an action is unsafe, unhealthy, not lawful, or violates the beliefs of the teen and his or her family. Naming the trouble allows the concerns to be clearly understood by both people.
3. **Identify the consequences.** Identifying the consequences reminds both people of what might result from the activity. It can open dialogue that will clarify positions and beliefs, increasing the opportunity for mutual understanding.
4. **Suggest alternatives.** Suggesting alternatives or other things to do demonstrates that the person saying no is still interested in the relationship, just not in the particular activity suggested. Alternative activities allow for a choice other than parting company.
5. **Move on.** Moving on removes a person from the immediate temptation and pressure and makes it clear that she or he really does mean no. It is also a call to the other person to choose to join in the alternative activity or be left behind.

These 5 refusal steps are logical and usually feel natural, but they do require understanding and practice to be used comfortably in real-life situations.

Final Evaluation

Final Evaluation

A Game and Puzzle Activity

For the final evaluation project, students create a brochure that will encourage and offer a plan to other students who want to practice abstinence.

Explain assignment

Invite students to produce a brochure that other students their age would find useful in making the choice to be abstinent. The brochure should contain the following parts:

- explanation of abstinence
- benefits of abstinence
- warnings about pressures to be sexually active
- descriptions of 2 skills that are helpful in being abstinent and examples of how to use them
- contract with a specific plan for choosing abstinence

Show model brochure (optional)

Show students *The Abstinence Contract* pamphlet (available from ETR Associates). This pamphlet presents a rationale and contract for abstinence for individuals and couples. It can serve as a model for student brochures.

Students create brochures

Distribute paper and art supplies and allow students time to work on their brochures, either individually or in small groups. Encourage students to use technology in their production, with computer layout, graphics and print, if these resources are available.

CRITERIA

Look for students' brochures to present the following:

- a clear definition of abstinence
- convincing arguments for the benefits of abstinence, including reference to:
  - — avoidance of pregnancy, STD and HIV
  - — better emotional health and growth
  - — development of stronger relationships
- a listing of possible pressures to be sexually active, including:
  - — media
  - — peers
  - — myths
  - — social stereotypes
  - — internal needs
- explanation of at least 2 of the following skills in relation to choosing abstinence:
  - — decision making
  - — STAR method
  - — communication—listening skills, I-statements, assertiveness
  - — refusal/delay skills
  - — specific plan for remaining abstinent and/or a contract for reader to sign

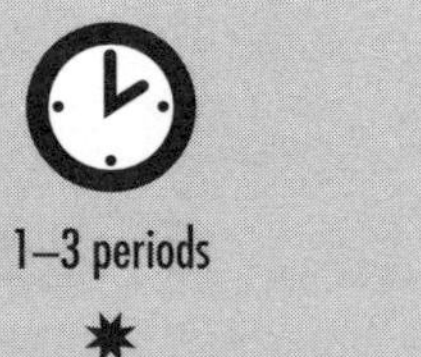

1–3 periods

✷

MATERIALS

- drawing paper
- art supplies
- *Optional: The Abstinence Contract* pamphlet
- *Optional:* technology resources

COMMUNITY LINK

Make arrangements for the completed brochures to actually be used or placed in areas where other students will have access to them. Brochures could be displayed at community outlets—other schools, health agencies, libraries, civic or church groups, etc.

Appendixes

Why Comprehensive School Health?

Components of a Comprehensive Health Program

The Teacher's Role

Teaching Strategies

Glossary

References

Why Comprehensive School Health?

The quality of life we ultimately achieve is determined in large part by the health decisions we make, the subsequent behaviors we adopt, and the public policies that promote and support the establishment of healthy behaviors.

A healthy student is capable of growing and learning; of producing new knowledge and ideas; of sharing, interacting and living peacefully with others in a complex and changing society. Fostering healthy children is the shared responsibility of families, communities and schools.

Health behaviors, the most important predictors of current and future health status, are influenced by a variety of factors. Factors that lead to and support the establishment of healthy behaviors include:

- awareness and knowledge of health issues
- the skills necessary to practice healthy behaviors
- opportunities to practice healthy behaviors
- support and reinforcement for the practice of healthy behaviors

The perception that a particular healthy behavior is worthwhile often results in young people becoming advocates, encouraging others to adopt the healthy behavior. When these young advocates exert pressure on peers to adopt healthy behaviors, a healthy social norm is established (e.g., tobacco use is unacceptable in this school).

Because health behaviors are learned, they can be shaped and changed. Partnerships between family members, community leaders, teachers and school leaders are a vital key to the initial development and maintenance of children's healthy behaviors and can also play a role in the modification of unhealthy behaviors. Schools, perhaps more than any other single agency in our society, have the opportunity to influence factors that shape the future health and productivity of Americans.

When young people receive reinforcement for the practice of a healthy behavior, they feel good about the healthy behavior. Reinforcement and the subsequent good feeling increase the likelihood that an individual will continue to practice a behavior and thereby establish a positive health habit. The good feeling and the experience of success motivate young people to place a high value on the behavior (e.g., being a nonsmoker is good).

From *Step by Step to Comprehensive School Health,* W. M. Kane (Santa Cruz, CA: ETR Associates, 1992).

Components of a Comprehensive Health Program

The school's role in fostering the development of healthy students involves more than providing classes in health. There are 8 components of a comprehensive health education program:

- **School Health Instruction**—Instruction is the in-class aspect of the program. As in other subject areas, a scope of content defines the field. Application of classroom instruction to real life situations is critical.
- **Healthy School Environment**—The school environment includes both the physical and psychological surroundings of students, faculty and staff. The physical environment should be free of hazards; the psychological environment should foster healthy development.
- **School Health Services**—School health services offer a variety of activities that address the health status of students and staff.
- **Physical Education and Fitness**—Participation in physical education and fitness activities promotes healthy development. Students need information about how and why to be active and encouragement to develop skills that will contribute to fitness throughout their lives.
- **School Nutrition and Food Services**—The school's nutritional program provides an excellent opportunity to model healthy behaviors. Schools that provide healthy food choices and discourage availability of unhealthy foods send a clear message to students about the importance of good nutrition.
- **School-Based Counseling and Personal Support**—School counseling and support services play an important role in responding to special needs and providing personal support for individual students, teachers and staff. These services can also provide programs that promote schoolwide mental, emotional and social well-being.
- **Schoolsite Health Promotion**—Health promotion is a combination of educational, organizational and environmental activities designed to encourage students and staff to adopt healthier lifestyles and become better consumers of health care services. It views the school and its activities as a total environment.
- **School, Family and Community Health Promotion Partnerships**—Partnerships that unite schools, families and communities can address communitywide issues. These collaborative partnerships are the cornerstone of health promotion and disease prevention.

The Teacher's Role

The teacher plays a critical role in meeting the challenge to empower students with the knowledge, skills and ability to make healthy behavior choices throughout their lives.

Instruction

Teachers need to provide students with learning opportunities that go beyond knowledge. Instruction must include the chance to practice skills that will help students make healthy decisions.

Involve Families and Communities

The issues in health are real-life issues, issues that families and communities deal with daily. Students need to see the relationship of what they learn at school to what occurs in their homes and their communities.

Model Healthy Behavior

Teachers educate students by their actions too. Students watch the way teachers manage health issues in their own lives. Teachers need to ask themselves if they are modeling the health behaviors they want students to adopt.

Maintain a Healthy Environment

The classroom environment has both physical and emotional aspects. It is the teacher's role to maintain a safe physical environment. It is also critical to provide an environment that is sensitive, respectful and developmentally appropriate.

Establish Groundrules

It is very important to establish classroom groundrules before discussing sensitive topics or issues. Setting and consistently enforcing groundrules establishes an atmosphere of respect, in which students can share and explore their personal thoughts, feelings, opinions and values.

Refer Students to Appropriate Services

Teachers may be the first to notice illness, learning disorders or emotional distress in students. The role of the teacher is one of referral. Most districts have guidelines for teachers to follow.

Legal Compliance

Teachers must make every effort to communicate to parents and other family members about the nature of the curriculum. Instruction about certain topics, such as sexuality, HIV or drug use, often must follow notification guidelines regulated by state law. Most states also require teachers to report any suspected cases of child abuse or neglect.

Teaching Strategies

The resource books incorporate a variety of instructional strategies. This variety is essential in addressing the needs of different kinds of learners. Different strategies are grouped according to their general education purpose. When sequenced, these strategies are designed to help students acquire the knowledge and skills they need to choose healthy behavior. Strategies are identified with each activity. Some strategies are traditional, while others are more interactive, encouraging students to help each other learn.

The strategies are divided into 4 categories according to their general purpose:

- providing key information
- encouraging creative expression
- sharing thoughts, feelings and opinions
- developing critical thinking

The following list details strategies in each category.

Providing Key Information

Information provides the foundation for learning. Before students can move to higher-level thinking, they need to have information about a topic. In lieu of a textbook, this series uses a variety of strategies to provide students the information they need to take actions for their health.

Anonymous Question Box

An anonymous question box provides the opportunity for all students to get answers to questions they might be hesitant to ask in class. It also gives teachers time to think about answers to difficult questions or to look for more information.

Questions should be reviewed and responded to regularly, and all questions placed in the box should be taken seriously. If you don't know the answer to a question, research it and report back to students.

You may feel that some questions would be better answered privately. Offer students the option of signing their questions if they want a private, written answer. Any questions not answered in class can then be answered privately.

Current Events

Analyzing local, state, national and international current events helps students relate classroom discussion to everyday life. It also helps students understand how local, national and global events and policies affect health status. Resources for current events include newspapers, magazines and other periodicals, radio and television programs and news.

Demonstrations and Experiments

Teachers, guest speakers or students can use demonstrations and experiments to show how something works or why something is important. These activities also provide a way to show the correct process for doing something, such as a first-aid procedure.

Demonstrations and experiments should be carefully planned and conducted. They often involve the use of supporting materials.

Games and Puzzles

Games and puzzles can be used to provide a different environment in which learning can take place. They are frequently amusing and sometimes competitive.

Many types of games and puzzles can be adapted to present and review health concepts. It may be a simple question-and-answer game or an adaptation of games such as Bingo, Concentration or Jeopardy. Puzzles include crosswords and word searches.

A game is played according to a specific set of rules. Game rules should be clear and simple. Using groups of students in teams rather than individual contestants helps involve the entire class.

Guest Speakers

Guest speakers can be recruited from students' families, the school and the community. They provide a valuable link between the classroom and the "real world."

Speakers should be screened before being invited to present to the class. They should have some awareness of the level of student knowledge and should be given direction for the content and focus of the presentation.

Interviewing

Students can interview experts and others about a specific topic either inside or outside of class. Invite experts, family members and others to visit class, or ask students to interview others (family members or friends) outside of class.

Advance preparation for an organized interview session increases the learning potential. A brainstorming session before the interview allows students to develop questions to ask during the interview.

Oral Presentations

Individual students or groups or panels of students can present information orally to the rest of the class. Such presentations may sometimes involve the use of charts or posters to augment the presentation.

Students enjoy learning and hearing from each other, and the experience stimulates positive interaction. It also helps build students' communication skills.

Encouraging Creative Expression

Student creativity should be encouraged and challenged. Creative expression provides the opportunity to integrate language arts, fine arts and personal experience into a lesson. It also helps meet the diverse needs of students with different learning styles.

Artistic Expression or Creative Writing

Students may be offered a choice of expressing themselves in art or through writing. They may write short stories, poems or letters, or create pictures or collages about topics they are studying. Such a choice accommodates the differing needs and talents of students.

This technique can be used as a follow-up to most lessons. Completed work should be displayed in the classroom, at school or in the community.

Dramatic Presentations

Dramatic presentations may take the form of skits or mock news, radio or television shows. They can be presented to the class or to larger groups in the school or community. When equipment is available, videotapes of these presentations provide an opportunity to present students' work to other classes in the school and other groups in the community.

Such presentations are highly motivating activities, because they actively involve students in learning desired concepts. They also allow students to practice new behaviors in a safe setting and help them personalize information presented in class.

Roleplays

Acting out difficult situations provides students practice in new behaviors in a safe setting. Sometimes students are given a part to play, and other times they are given an idea and asked to improvise. Students need time to decide the central action of the situation and how they will resolve it before they make their presentation. Such activities are highly motivating because they actively involve students in learning desired concepts or practicing certain behaviors.

Sharing Thoughts, Feelings and Opinions

In the sensitive areas of health education, students may have a variety of opinions and feelings. Providing a safe atmosphere in which to discuss opinions and feelings encourages students to share their ideas and listen and learn from others. Such discussion also provides an opportunity to clarify misinformation and correct misconceptions.

Brainstorming

Brainstorming is used to stimulate discussion of an issue or topic. It can be done with the whole class or in smaller groups. It can be used both to gather information and to share thoughts and opinions.

All statements should be accepted without comment or judgment from the teacher or other students. Ideas can be listed on the board, on butcher paper or newsprint or on a transparency. Brainstorming should continue until all ideas have been exhausted or a predetermined time limit has been reached.

Class Discussion

A class discussion led by the teacher or by students is a valuable educational strategy. It can be used to initiate, amplify or summarize a lesson. Such discussions also provide a way to share ideas, opinions and concerns that may have been generated in small group work.

Clustering

Clustering is a simple visual technique that involves diagraming ideas around a main topic. The main topic is written on the board and circled. Other related ideas are then attached to the central idea or to each other with connecting lines.

Clustering can be used as an adjunct to brainstorming. Because there is no predetermined number of secondary ideas, clustering can accommodate all brainstorming ideas.

Continuum Voting

Continuum voting is a stimulating discussion technique. Students express the extent to which they agree or disagree with a statement read by the teacher. The classroom should be prepared for this activity with a sign that says "Agree" on one wall and a sign that says "Disagree" on the opposite wall. There should be room for students to move freely between the 2 signs.

As the teacher reads a statement, students move to a point between the signs that reflects their thoughts or feelings. The closer to the "Agree" sign they stand, the stronger their agreement. The closer to the "Disagree" sign they stand, the stronger their disagreement. A position in the center between the signs indicates a neutral stance.

Dyad Discussion

Working in pairs allows students to provide encouragement and support to each other. Students who may feel uncomfortable sharing in the full class may be more willing to share their thoughts and feelings with 1 other person. Depending on the task, dyads may be temporary, or students may meet regularly with a partner and work together to achieve their goals.

Forced Field Analysis

This strategy is used to discuss an issue that is open to debate. Students analyze a situation likely to be approved by some students and opposed by others. For example, if the subject of discussion was the American diet, some students might support the notion that Americans consume healthy foods because of the wide variety of foods available. Other students might express concern about the amount of foods that are high in sodium, fat and sugar.

Questioning skills are critical to the success of this technique. A good way to open such a discussion is to ask students, "What questions should you ask to determine if you support or oppose this idea?" The pros and cons of students' analysis can be charted on the board or on a transparency.

Journal Writing

Journal writing affords the opportunity for thinking and writing. Expressive writing requires that students become actively involved in the learning process. However, writing may become a less effective tool for learning if students must worry about spelling and punctuation. Students should be encouraged to write freely in their journals, without fear of evaluation.

Panel Discussion

Panel discussions provide an opportunity to discuss different points of view about a health topic, problem or issue. Students can research and develop supporting arguments for different sides. Such research and discussion enhances understanding of content.

Panel members may include experts from the community as well as students. Panel discussions are usually directed by a moderator and may be followed by a question and answer period.

Self-Assessment

Personal inventories provide a tool for self-assessment. Providing privacy around personal assessments allows students to be honest in their responses. Volunteers can share answers or the questions can be discussed in general, but no students should have to share answers they would prefer to keep private. Students can use the information to set personal goals for changing behaviors.

Small Groups

Students working together can help stimulate each other's creativity. Small group activities are cooperative, but have less formal structure than cooperative learning groups. These activities encourage collective thinking and provide opportunities for students to work with others and increase social skills.

Surveys and Inventories

Surveys and inventories can be used to assess knowledge, attitudes, beliefs and practices. These instruments can be used to gather knowledge about a variety of groups, including students, parents and other family members, and teachers.

Students can use surveys others have designed or design their own. When computers are available, students can use them to summarize their information, create graphs and prepare presentations of the data.

Developing Critical Thinking

Critical thinking skills help students analyze health topics and issues. These activities require that students learn to gather information, consider the consequences of actions and behaviors and make responsible decisions. They challenge students to perform higher-level thinking and clearly communicate their ideas.

Case Studies

Case studies provide written histories of a problem or situation. Students can read, discuss and analyze these situations. This strategy encourages student involvement and helps students personalize the health-related concepts presented in class.

Teaching Strategies

Cooperative Learning Groups

Cooperative learning is an effective teaching strategy that has been shown to have a positive effect on students' achievement and interpersonal skills. Students can work in small groups to disseminate and share information, analyze ideas or solve problems. The size of the group depends on the nature of the lesson and the make-up of the class. Groups work best with from 2–6 members.

Group structure will affect the success of the lessons. Groups can be formed by student choice, random selection, or a more formal, teacher-influenced process. Groups seem to function best when they represent the variety and balance found in the classroom. Groups also work better when each student has a responsibility within the group (reader, recorder, timer, reporter, etc.).

While groups are working on their tasks, the teacher should move from group to group, answering questions and dealing with any problems that arise. At the conclusion of the group process, some closure should take place.

Debates

Students can debate the pros and cons of many issues relating to health. Suggesting that students defend an opposing point of view provides an additional learning experience.

During a debate, each side has the opportunity to present their arguments and to refute each others' arguments. After the debate, class members can choose the side with which they agree.

Factual Writing

Once students have been presented with information about a topic, a variety of writing assignments can challenge them to clarify and express their ideas and opinions. Position papers, letters to the editor, proposals and public service announcements provide a forum in which students can express their opinions, supporting them with facts, figures and reasons.

Media Analysis

Students can analyze materials from a variety of media, including printed matter, music, TV programs, movies, video games and advertisements, to identify health-related messages. Such analysis might include identifying the purpose of the piece, the target audience, underlying messages, motivations and stereotypes.

Personal Contracts

Personal contracts, individual commitments to changing behavior, can help students make positive changes in their health-related behaviors. The wording of a personal contract may include the behavior to be changed, a plan for changing the behavior and the identification of possible problems and support systems.

However, personal contracts should be used with caution. Behavior change may be difficult, especially in the short term. Students should be encouraged to make personal contracts around goals they are likely to meet.

Research

Research requires students to seek information to complete a task. Students may be given prepared materials that they must use to complete an assignment, or they may have to locate resources and gather information on their own. As part of this strategy, students must compile and organize the information they collect.

Glossary

A

abstain—To refrain from doing something by one's own choice.

abstinence—Avoiding sexual intercourse by one's own choice.

adolescence—The period between sexual maturity at puberty and the attainment of adult social status; psychosocial development during the teenage years.

adulthood—The state of being mature in years, of having grown to full size and strength.

affection—Fond or tender feeling; warm liking.

age of consent—In law, the age of a girl before which sexual intercourse with her, regardless of whether she has consented, is considered rape.

aggressive—Hostile, demanding, pushy or demeaning of others.

analysis—The process of studying something to determine its features and relationships.

appropriate—Suitable for a particular occasion or situation.

assertiveness—A component of communication in which individuals stand up for what they believe, want or need, without hurting or denying the rights of others.

B

biological—Having to do with living matter, plant or animal; having to do with the physical part of a person.

body language—A form of nonverbal communication made up of facial expressions, body movement, posture, gestures, etc., that are clues to a person's thoughts and feelings.

C

celibate—Abstaining from sexual intercourse, especially for reason of religious vows.

chlamydia—Any of several common, often asymptomatic, sexually transmitted diseases caused by a microorganism.

comfortable—At ease in body or mind.

communication—The ability to express thoughts, feelings and reactions and to exchange information among people through a common system of symbols, signs or behaviors.

consequence—The result of an action.

continence—Self-restraint in sexual activity; abstinence.

contract—An agreement between 2 or more people to do something.

Glossary

cultural—Having to do with the effect that behavior patterns, arts, beliefs and institutions in society have on people.

culture—Ideas, customs, skills and arts of a people or group.

D

decision—The result of making up one's mind; a judgment or conclusion.

decision making—Making choices; using one's own judgment.

delay—To put off to a later time.

delaying tactics—Techniques that give a person time to decide what to do or how to refuse.

E

emotions—Feelings about or reactions to certain important events or thoughts.

ethical—In accordance with accepted principles of right and wrong; moral.

exploitation—Using another person for selfish purposes.

external pressure—Pressure from outside sources, e.g., family, peers, society.

F

facial expression—How the features of the face respond to emotions; a nonverbal gesture or clue that can convey how a person feels or thinks about a certain topic, idea or emotion.

fondling—Stroking or caressing lovingly.

G

gender identity—The personal, internal sense of oneself as male or female.

genitals—The male or female sex organs.

goal—An end that a person aims to reach or accomplish.

goal setting—Making plans for the future.

H

heterosexual—Feeling sexual attraction toward persons of the other sex.

HIV (human immunodeficiency virus)—The virus that causes AIDS.

homosexual—Feeling sexual attraction toward persons of the same sex.

hormone—A chemical substance secreted by an endocrine gland and transported in the blood or other body fluids to stimulate growth and regulate body functions.

Glossary

I

inappropriate—Not suitable for a particular occasion or situation.

influence—The ability of a person or group to affect others; someone or something that affects others.

internal pressure—Pressure from inside sources, e.g., personal beliefs, thoughts, attitudes.

intimacy—A state of connectedness and trust between people.

intimate—Most private or personal; very close.

I-statement—A way to express thoughts, feelings and needs while respecting the rights of other.

L

love—Strong affection or liking for someone or something.

M

masturbation—Touching one's own sex organs for sexual pleasure.

media—All the means of communication that provide the public with news and entertainment, including newspapers, radio and TV.

mental/emotional effects—The influence something has on a person's feelings of love, hate, fear or anger.

model—An example to be imitated or compared.

myth—A belief that is untrue or not always true.

N

necking—Kissing and petting.

nocturnal emission—Wet dream; orgasm with ejaculation that occurs during sleep.

norms—Standards or rules for behavior.

O

orgasm—Climactic, satisfying response to sexual stimulation, marking the sudden discharge of accumulated sexual tension.

outercourse—Physical behaviors that do not include sexual intercourse; hugging, kissing, holding one another.

Glossary

P

passion—A powerful emotion such as love, joy, hatred, anger or greed; strong sexual desire.

passive—Submissive, inactive, yielding to others.

peer power—Friends influencing friends to choose healthy behaviors.

peer pressure—The influence of friends on behavior; can have positive or negative results.

peers—People of the same or similar age who are similar in many ways.

petting—Caressing and kissing.

plan—A scheme for making, doing or arranging something; a project; a program; a schedule.

pregnancy—The conception and carrying of a fetus to term.

premarital—Before marriage.

pressure—Strong influence.

pressure lines—Statements used to persuade individuals to engage in specific activities.

psychological—Having to do with the mind, both normal and abnormal states; having to do with the mental part of a person that determines attitudes.

psychosocial—Involving aspects of both social and psychological behavior.

puberty—Stage of life in which the reproductive system matures and secondary sex characteristics appear.

R

refusal skills—Methods of declining to do something or rejecting what is offered.

reproduction—The sexual process by which people make babies.

reward—Something received in return for a action; the benefit of taking a risk.

risk—The likelihood of injury, damage or other negative consequences following an action.

risky behaviors—Actions that cause an increased likelihood of injury, damage or other negative consequences.

S

safe—Free from damage, danger or injury.

secure—Free from danger; safe; not worried or troubled.

self-control—Ability to control behavior or expression of emotions.

self-efficacy—The perception that one is able to use one's skills to master a task.

self-esteem—Measure of how much a person values himself or herself.

Glossary

self-image—One's concept of oneself or one's status.
self-monitoring—The process of thinking through an intended behavior change, setting specific goals and assessing progress toward achieving them.
sex—Used to refer to sexual actions, such as sexual intercourse.
sexual intercourse—A type of contact involving 1 of the following: (1) insertion of a man's penis into a woman's vagina (vaginal intercourse); (2) placement of the mouth on the genitals of another person (oral intercourse) or (3) insertion of a man's penis into the anus of another person (anal intercourse).
sexuality—The part of a person's personality that has to do with all aspects of being male or female.
sexually transmitted disease (STD)—Any of a number of diseases that can spread through sexual contact.
stereotype—Standardized image or conception.
stress management—Dealing with pressures and anxieties.
syphilis—A sexually transmitted disease caused by bacteria.

T

target audience—The population or group of people for whom a particular campaign or message is intended.
temptation—The opportunity to do something risky.

U

unsafe—Dangerous; risky.

V

values—Beliefs or qualities that are important, desirable or prized.
virgin—A person who has not experienced sexual intercourse.

Y

you-statement—Message that blames others for actions or results.

References

Archer, D., D. Kimes and M. Barrios. 1978. Face-ism. *Psychology Today* (September): 65-66.

Barth, R. P. 1996. *Reducing the risk: Building skills to prevent pregnancy, STD & HIV.* 3d ed. Santa Cruz, CA: ETR Associates.

Bruess, C. E., and J. S. Greenberg. 1988. *Sexuality education theory and practice.* 2d ed. New York: Macmillan.

Campbell, B. 1994. *The multiple intelligences handbook.* Standwood, WA: Campbell and Associates.

Core-Gebhard, P, and M. Young. 1994. *Sex can wait: An abstinence-based sexuality curriculum for high school.* Santa Cruz, CA: ETR Associates.

Cox, F. 1978. *Human intimacy: Marriage, the family and its meaning.* St. Paul, MN: West.

Drolet, J. C., and K. Clark. 1994. *The sexuality education challenge: Promoting healthy sexuality in young people.* Santa Cruz, CA: ETR Associates.

Erickson, E. 1963. *Childhood and society.* New York: W. Norton.

Fetro, J. V. 1992. *Personal & social skills: Understanding and integrating competencies across health content.* Santa Cruz, CA: ETR Associates.

Jensen, E. P. 1988. *Super teaching master strategies for building student success.* Del Mar, CA: Turning Points.

Levine, L., and L. Barbach. 1983. *The intimate male: Candid discussions about women, sex and relationships.* New York: Doubleday.

Meeks, L., and P. Heit. 1992. *Comprehensive school health education: Totally awesome strategies for teaching health.* Blacklick, OH: Meeks Heit.

Snegroff, S. 1986. The stressors of non-marital sexual intercourse. *Health Education* 17:21-23.

Stang, L., and K. R. Miner. 1994. *Sexuality: Health facts.* Santa Cruz, CA: ETR Associates.

Taylor, M. E., and D. Adame. 1986. Male and female sexuality attitudes: Differences and similarities. *Health Education* 17:8-12.

Thacker, N. L., and K. R. Miner. 1994. *Abstinence: Health facts*. Santa Cruz, CA: ETR Associates.

MASTERS

CONTENTS

Dimensions of Sexuality

Name ______________________________ Date ______________ Period ______

Biological	Psychological
Sexuality	
Cultural	Ethical

MYTH

Definition:

Example:

Why is this a myth?

What problems could this myth cause for people or society?

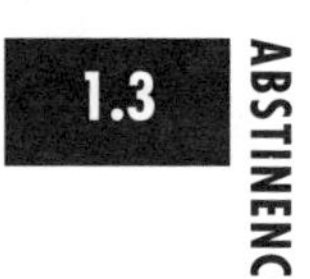

Myths About Sexuality

Student Reading

Myths About Sexuality

People may put a lot of pressure on themselves to have sex because of myths they believe about sex. A myth is a widely held belief that is untrue or may not always be true. If there are exceptions to a statement, even though it is popularly held to be true, it is a myth.

Believing myths can cause us to act or not act in a certain way. The need to belong and to be accepted can cause us to accept a myth we think others believe. Myths about sex can influence the sexual choices we make for ourselves.

One example of a sexual myth is that "Everyone is doing it." This belief is obviously a myth. Many teenagers (and adults) choose not to have sex—some because of circumstances or lack of opportunity, but many others because of personal values or concerns. Even though this statement is not true, believing it can cause teens to feel pressure to become or to continue to be sexually active.

Many myths develop as a result of media depictions of sex. The media often show sex as ideal, romantic, sensual, loving and joyous. Though this can certainly be true in the right setting, with the right person and at the right time of life, it is not always true. The desire for this ideal experience adds to pressures people may feel about having sex.

Believing in sexual myths can pressure people into being sexually active. This can prove harmful both physically and emotionally. A person's self-esteem, relationships, health and future can suffer if he or she becomes sexually active at the wrong time in life. Sexual relationships must be built on trust and mature love that takes time to develop, or they can prove damaging to the relationship and the individuals.

Recognizing a statement as a myth can reduce the influence it has on a person's decisions and actions.

Common Sexual Myths

Here are some common myths about sex and sexuality.

Having sex shows a couple is really in love. *While having sex can be an expression of love, it doesn't really prove a couple is in love. Couples have sex for many reasons other than being in love. Some people have sex for physical pleasure, some because of curiosity, some to prove that they are sexually normal, some because their partner pressures them into it, and some because the pressure of society makes them think they should. It is possible for couples to express their love in many ways that do not include sexual intercourse.*

Most teens are sexually active. *In fact, many teens choose to wait to have sex. About half of the students in grades 9-12 have never had sexual intercourse and many of those who have do not have sex regularly. Of those who have had sexual intercourse, many wish they had waited.*

If a person has had sex once, there's no reason to say no to having sex again. *Many people have sex once and decide they don't want to keep having it. They choose to become abstinent again. Sometimes they decide that sex was not like they had pictured it. They may be worried about pregnancy, disease or emotional strain and feel it's just not worth the risk. Some find that their moral or religious beliefs conflict with these actions. Some decide they want sex to be more special and choose to wait until they find the right person.*

Boys need to have sex more than girls. *There is no evidence to support this statement. Sex drive is not determined by gender. The desire to have sex varies from person to person and is dependent on many different things. Some women's choice to be abstinent may be due to fear of pregnancy or disease or many other reasons, not a lower sex drive. This myth is promoted in our society, which*

(continued...)

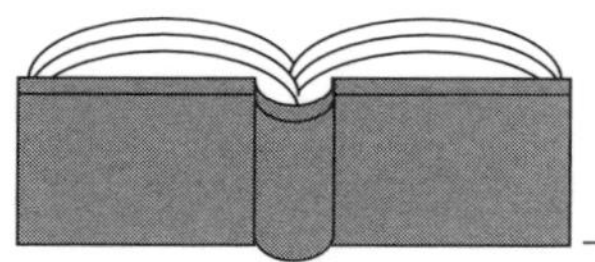

Myths About Sexuality

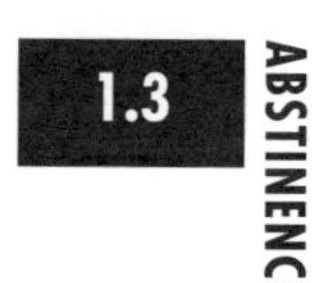

Student Reading, Continued

often sets a double standard where sexual activity is accepted or even encouraged for men yet frowned upon for women.

One way to keep a boyfriend or girlfriend is to have sex. *Having sex doesn't guarantee a boyfriend or girlfriend will stay. Having sex can put too much pressure on the relationship. Sometimes having sex will make a partner stay for a time out of a sense of duty or guilt; but a relationship might also end after having sex because the challenge is gone or because a partner feels tied down and doesn't want to be. The better way to keep a boyfriend or girlfriend is to spend time together, doing things you both enjoy and building closeness and trust.*

The best way to get to know someone is to have sex with him or her. *Having sex is only 1 way of getting to know someone. There are many facets of a person's character one does not learn about during sex. If sex replaces talking, spending time with mutual friends and enjoying activities together, a couple may never truly get to know each other.*

Having sex will make a relationship better. *Having sex too early may actually harm a relationship. If either partner does not feel ready for sex or feels pressured into having sex, it can damage feelings of trust and be a barrier to intimacy. Protection from pregnancy and STD are also important. If a couple can't discuss sex with each other they're not ready for it. Good sex requires trust and intimacy, which can take a long time to develop.*

Teens who are still virgins when they graduate from high school are probably gay or lesbian. *Many heterosexual people don't have sex until after high school because they believe they should wait for marriage, or have other strong beliefs about when sex will be appropriate, and control their sexual desires until then. Some gay and lesbian teens may be sexually active in high school just as some heterosexual teens are. There is really no difference in the choices of heterosexual and gay or lesbian teens in this respect. Studies show that delaying sex is not related to sexual orientation but to religious beliefs and life goals.*

Messages About Sex—Family Page

This activity gives you an opportunity to be sure the messages your son or daughter receives from you are the messages you intend to give.

Part 1

Ask your son or daughter to complete his or her activity sheet while you do yours. Write 3 messages about sex that you think you have given your child. These messages may have been stated verbally or given by example through the way you live your life and express your sexuality.

My 3 messages:

1.

2.

3.

Part 2

With your son or daughter, read the messages you have written. Ask if he or she has clearly understood your messages.

Read the messages written by your son or daughter. Discuss whether these were messages you intended to give. Did your child clearly and completely understand your messages? If they were not the messages you intended to give, discuss how your child perceived them and how the misunderstood message differs from your actual belief.

When you are finished, please complete the **Messages About Sex—Feedback Form**, sign it and send it to school with your son or daughter as evidence of completion of the activity.

Messages About Sex—Student Page

This activity gives you an opportunity to be sure the messages you receive from the adults in your family are the messages they intend to give.

Part 1

Complete this activity sheet while your parent or other adult family member does his or hers. Write 3 messages your family has given you about sex. The messages may be actual things family members have said, or messages you haven't actually heard but think your family believes. You may have received the message from observing your family's behavior.

My 3 messages:

1.

2.

3.

Part 2

When you and an adult family member have both written 3 messages, follow the steps in Part 2 of the **Messages About Sex—Family Page.**

Messages About Sex—Feedback Form

DIRECTIONS Your evaluation of this activity will help us as we work to bring families and the school closer together. Please respond to the following questions about this activity. Then sign the form and have your child return it to school as evidence of completion of the activity.

	very worthwhile				not at all worthwhile
Overall rating of this activity (circle one):	1	2	3	4	5

In what way was this activity worthwhile?

In what way was it *not* worthwhile?

Was any portion of this activity too difficult? How?

What suggestions do you have for improving this activity?

____________________ Adult signature

____________________ Student signature

__________ Date

Reflecting on Sexuality and Myths

1.7

ABSTINENCE

Name ______________________ Date ______________ Period ______

DIRECTIONS Write your responses to the following questions.

1. Sexuality is a normal and healthy part of personality. What are some of the influences on the development of this part of your personality? (List and explain up to 6.)

2. A myth is a statement that is not always true but is accepted as true by some people. How can a myth about sex influence a person's sexual attitudes and behavior?

3. How will you be able to use this knowledge in your life?

Sexuality Pressures

Name ______________________ Date ______________ Period ______

Internal	External
Internal pressure is…	**External pressure is…**
Some internal pressures that influence me:	**Some external pressures that influence me:**

Media Analysis Project

Name ______________________________ Date ______________ Period ______

DIRECTIONS The purpose of this project is to gather evidence of how the media use sex and how that can influence teens. You will gather evidence by researching your assigned form of media. Then your group will create a poster to show your resources and examples of your evidence and complete a report about your findings. The group reporter will present the findings in a panel discussion.

Group members' names: ______________________________

Media assignment: ______________________________

Step 1: Assign Jobs

Researchers:

- All group members will gather research.

Research Director: ______________________________

- Responsible for designing research, assigning research work to other members and collecting the results. Organizing skills needed.

Art Director: ______________________________

- Responsible for creating the poster showing the evidence and conclusions. Creative and artistic skills needed.

Writer: ______________________________

- Responsible for producing the final written copy of the group report. Typing/writing skills needed.

Reporter: ______________________________

- Responsible for reporting findings to the class as part of the discussion panel. Good speaking skills needed.

(continued...)

Media Analysis Project

Continued

Step 2: Design Research Process

The *Research Director* will lead the group in choosing what material from this media will be observed and who will do it. Each *Researcher* will complete the **Media Research Observation Form** and return it to the *Research Director.*

Some ideas for research include:

- TV: Make a list of programs to review and who will watch each one.
- Magazines: Make a list of the magazines to review and who will read each one.
- Movies: Make a list of the movies to review and who will see each one.
- Music video: Make a list of the videos to review and who will watch each one.
- Music: Make a list of the groups/songs to review and who will listen to each one.
- Radio: Make a list of the stations/DJs to review and who will listen to each one.

Step 3: Gather Evidence

Each *Researcher* will gather evidence that demonstrates the use of sex in the media. The *Art Director* will take these items and use them in the poster. Some ideas for evidence to gather include:

- TV: Get *TV Guide* listing of program description. Create or cut out art to represent the program.
- Magazine: Cut out examples of advertising, cover picture, articles, etc.
- Movie: Cut out newspaper advertising for the movie. Create art or cut out to represent the movie.
- Music video: Make copies of the pictures on the cover. Create or cut out art to represent the video.
- Music: Make copies of the CD or cassette cover. Write out the lyrics. Create or cut out art to represent the theme or words of the music.
- Radio: Create or cut out artwork to represent the music or commercials played. Get advertising pictures from the station.

(continued...)

Media Analysis Project

Continued

Step 4: Create Presentation

Your group will meet to bring all **Media Research Observation Forms** and evidence together. All *Researchers* will help in the following jobs wherever they are needed.

- The *Research Director* will lead the discussion on the research questions.
- The *Writer* will take notes and write the **Media Influence Report** for the group, including the conclusions for the poster.
- The *Art Director* will collect all of the evidence and create an attractive poster to demonstrate the conclusions.
- The *Reporter* will prepare to present the poster of evidence, the **Media Influence Report** and the group's conclusions as part of a class panel discussion.

Step 5: Materials to Be Completed

- **Media Research Observation Form** from each group member
- **Media Influence Report** from the *Writer*
- poster of evidence and conclusions created by the *Art Director*

Media Influence Report

Name ______________________ Date ______________ Period ______

Reported by: ______________________

Group members: ______________________

Medium researched: ______________________

Evidence collected from (list names of programs, magazines, songs, etc.):

How was sex included in this form of media?

Does this contribute to myths or stereotypes about sex? How?

What message does the use of sex in this form of media send to teens?

What is the likely effect of this message on teens' attitudes and sexual behaviors?

Conclusion

Write a statement saying how much influence you think this form of media has on teens' attitudes and sexual behaviors. Include this conclusion statement on your evidence poster.

Media Research Observation Form

Name ______________________________ Date ______________ Period ______

Assigned medium: ______________________________

Observation of (name of program, song, magazine, video, etc.):

What target audience is this intended for?

Describe what you observed.

How is sex included in what you observed?

STEREOTYPES OF MALES AND FEMALES

Name ______________________ Date ______________ Period ______

Definition of stereotype:

TYPICAL STEREOTYPES:	
MEN	WOMEN

Sexual stereotypes that cause the most pressure for teens:

Stereotype

Definition: A standard image of what a person should be or do.

Typical Stereotypes:	
Men	**Women**

Sexual stereotypes that could cause pressure toward sexual activity:

Media Messages—Family Page

This activity gives you an opportunity to discuss the messages about sexuality presented in the media and whether these messages are acceptable in your family.

Part 1

List 2 TV programs your son or daughter watches that you think present a strong message about sexuality. Write whether that message is positive or negative and why.

Note: If your family does not watch television, you could discuss the messages in movies your son or daughter has seen or popular magazines he or she reads.

Program 1: ______________________________

Positive or negative message? ______________________________

Why?

Program 2: ______________________________

Positive or negative message? ______________________________

Why?

Part 2

Compare your list and your reasons with those your daughter or son wrote. Do you agree? Watch the programs together this week and discuss your perceptions of the messages about sex and how you feel they may influence your son or daughter.

When you are finished, please complete the **Media Messages—Feedback Form**, sign it and send it to school with your son or daughter as evidence of completion of the activity.

MEDIA MESSAGES—STUDENT PAGE

This activity gives you an opportunity to share your thoughts about the programs you watch on TV and how these programs might influence your views of sex.

PART 1

List 2 TV programs that you watch that you think present a strong message about sexuality. Write whether that message is positive or negative and why.

Program 1: ______________________________

Positive or negative message? ______________________

Why?

Program 2: ______________________________

Positive or negative message? ______________________

Why?

PART 2

DIRECTIONS When you and an adult family member have both written about 2 programs, follow the steps in Part 2 of the **Media Messages—Family Page**.

Media Messages—Feedback Form

DIRECTIONS Your evaluation of this activity will help us as we work to bring families and the school closer together. Please respond to the following questions about this activity. Then sign the form and have your child return it to school as evidence of completion of the activity.

	very worthwhile				not at all worthwhile
Overall rating of this activity (circle one):	1	2	3	4	5

In what way was this activity worthwhile?

In what way was it *not* worthwhile?

Was any portion of this activity too difficult? How?

What suggestions do you have for improving this activity?

____________________ Adult signature

____________________ Student signature

__________ Date

Identifying Pressures

Name ______________________ Date ______________ Period ______

DIRECTIONS Answer these questions, giving your own opinion on each.

What are 2 strong *external* pressures to be sexually active that teens face?

What are 2 strong *internal* pressures to be sexually active that teens face?

What are 2 strong influences on teens to be abstinent?

How can teens increase the influences toward sexual responsibility in their lives?

Thrill Seekers List

3.1 ABSTINENCE

Name ______________________ Date ______________ Period _______

Discuss each risk behavior to determine a possible reward from this behavior and a possible consequence. Write these in the space provided.

Then cut along the lines to make separate strips. Discuss the consequences and rewards of each action to determine which carry the highest risks. Paste the strips on your poster in order, with the most risky ones toward the top and the least risky ones toward the bottom.

Not wearing a safety belt in a car.
Reward:
Consequence:

Walking alone at night.
Reward:
Consequence:

Smoking cigarettes.
Reward:
Consequence:

Being alone with your boyfriend/girlfriend so you can be sexually intimate.
Reward:
Consequence:

Riding in a car with a drunk driver.
Reward:
Consequence:

Having sex with no protection.
Reward:
Consequence:

Not wearing a helmet while riding a motorcycle.
Reward:
Consequence:

Having sex with someone you just met.
Reward:
Consequence:

Temptations

Name ______________________ Date ______________ Period ______

Situation	My Value	My "Rule"	Consequence	My Action
1. You don't know an answer on the math test, but you can see the answer sheet of Bill, the class "brain." (cheating)	Honesty	Do the best I can at the time.	If I cheat and get caught, I could flunk. Even if I don't get caught, I'll feel guilty.	Think as hard as I can. Do my best.
2. Megan is spreading rumors about you that have made you really angry. She says to meet her after school to "settle" things. (fighting)				
3. At a party, Danny gives you a beer and challenges you to chug it. (drinking)				
4. Chris and a group of friends are going to the park at noon. They say it's easy to cut class. (skipping class)				
5. Susie invites you to her room during a party. She says she wants to be alone with you. (sexual activity)				
6. Hal has invited you to go swimming at midnight when no one else will be around. (sexual activity)				
7. ____________ ____________ ____________				

5 Steps in Decision Making

Decision to be made:

____

1. **Gather information.**

2. **List possible actions.**

3. **List consequences of each action.**

4. **Choose the best action and try it.**

5. **Evaluate the outcome.**

Decision-Making Steps

Name ______________________ Date ____________ Period ______

Decision to be made: ______________________

1. Information: ______________________

2. Actions:

3. Consequences:

4. Choose 1 action:

5. Evaluate:

STAR

Stop

- Wait, I need to think this through!

Think

- Is it really worth it?
- How will I feel after I've done this?
- Could I or anyone else be harmed if I do this?
- What is the most honest, ethical thing to do?
- Does this fit with the rules I've made for myself?

Act

- I know what is best to do and I'll do it.

Review

- Did I make the right choice?
- What should I do if this situation comes up again?

STAR Cartoon

Name ______________________________ Date ______________ Period ______

DIRECTIONS Write in the thoughts and words that show how to use the 4 STAR steps—Stop, Think, Act, Review.

STAR Cartoon Example

Write in the thoughts and words that show how to use the 4 STAR steps—Stop, Think, Act, Review.

Are You Ready for Sex?—Family Page

This activity gives you and your son or daughter an opportunity to share your views and feelings about having sex as a teen. Realizing that sharing sexual intercourse with someone is a big step that has many consequences is an important part of making decisions about sex.

Part 1

Complete these questions while your son or daughter completes his or hers.

List 3 reasons you think teens choose to have sex:

1.

2.

3.

List 3 things you think teens need to think about before choosing to have sex:

1.

2.

3.

Explain your personal criteria for deciding when or if having sex is OK:

Part 2

DIRECTIONS Compare your answers with those of your daughter or son. Discuss how they are similar and how and why they are different.

When you are finished, please complete the **Are You Ready for Sex?—Feedback Form,** sign it and send it to school with your son or daughter as evidence of completion of the activity.

Are You Ready for Sex?—Student Page

Realizing that sharing sexual intercourse with someone is a big step that has many consequences is an important part of making decisions about sex. This activity gives you an opportunity to share with your family your ideas about having sex as a teen.

Part 1

Complete these questions while your parent or other adult family member completes his or hers.

List 3 reasons you think teens choose to have sex:

1.

2.

3.

List 3 things you think teens need to think about before choosing to have sex:

1.

2.

3.

Explain your personal criteria for deciding when or if having sex is OK:

Part 2

DIRECTIONS When you are both finished, follow the steps in Part 2 of the **Are You Ready for Sex?—Family Page.**

Are You Ready for Sex?— Feedback Form

Your evaluation of this activity will help us as we work to bring families and the school closer together. Please respond to the following questions about this activity. Then sign the form and have your child return it to school as evidence of completion of the activity.

	very worthwhile				not at all worthwhile
Overall rating of this activity (circle one):	1	2	3	4	5

In what way was this activity worthwhile?

In what way was it *not* worthwhile?

Was any portion of this activity too difficult? How?

What suggestions do you have for improving this activity?

____________________	____________________	__________
Adult signature	Student signature	Date

EVALUATING RISKS AND DECISIONS

Name ________________________ Date ______________ Period _______

DIRECTIONS Choose 1 of these situations that could lead to sexual activity. Answer the questions based on this situation.

SITUATION 1

Shari and John come home to Shari's house after seeing a romantic movie. It's about 10:00 p.m. Shari's parents have left a note saying that they are visiting friends and won't be home until after midnight. The house is empty and quiet. Shari and John put some soft music on and begin to dance slowly. They are both beginning to be sexually excited.

SITUATION 2

Kim and Chris have been to a party where they both had something to drink. They stop the car on a quiet dead-end road to talk. Talking leads to touching, which leads to kissing, which gets pretty intense.

SITUATION 3

Robin's family is gone for the weekend. Robin invited some friends over for a late night swim. They have some beer and someone gets the idea to skinny dip.

Situation ______________________________________

What is the **risk behavior** that is tempting in this situation?

What is the possible **reward** of this behavior?

What is the possible **consequence** of this behavior?

Based on your decisions about sex, what is your **"rule"** concerning this behavior?

Write the dialog you might use in the **STAR method.**

S TOP:

T ________:

A ________:

R ________:

Listening: An Important Skill

Good Listening

- Facing the speaker.
- Making eye contact.
- Paying close attention.
- Giving nonverbal feedback to show you are listening, e.g., nod head.
- Asking questions to clarify as needed.
- Trying to understand the feelings of the speaker.
- Not allowing your personal views to affect your understanding.

Poor Listening

- Sitting facing away from the speaker.
- Looking around the room, not at the speaker.
- Body language that says you are not interested.
- Doing something else while trying to listen.
- Interrupting in the middle of an idea.
- Making unrelated remarks.
- Changing the subject before the speaker is finished.
- Talking to someone else while the speaker is talking.
- Trying to top the speaker's story with one of your own.
- Thinking about how you will respond before you hear all the speaker has to say.
- Putting the speaker down because you don't agree.

"I" and "You" Statements

You-statement: "You are so irresponsible. You are always late and now you're making me late!"

I-statement: "I depend on you to pick me up on time to get to practice. If I'm late, I get in trouble. I feel angry because I was ready on time."

The Parts of an I-Statement

1. **Behavior:** Name the behavior.
   Example: "I depend on you to pick me up on time to get to practice."
2. **Effect:** Explain how the behavior affects you.
   Example: "If I'm late I get in trouble."
3. **Feeling:** Explain how you feel.
   Example: "I feel angry because I was ready on time."

Practice for I-Statements

- Your friend takes you out to lunch and eats so slowly that you are late for math class.
  Example: Lunch took so long that I was late for math class and had to go to detention. I felt embarrassed.
- Your good friend is angry with Terry, who is also a friend of yours. Your friend often starts saying critical things about Terry to you.
  Example: I understand that you are angry with Terry and want to talk about it, but Terry is also a friend of mine. I feel uncomfortable because I feel caught in the middle between you and Terry.
- You practiced and know your lines for the play, but the person you have a scene with still doesn't know her lines.
  Example: I've noticed you have to look at the script a lot during rehearsal. It's hard for me to do our scene when you don't know the lines. I feel frustrated because I want our scene to go well.

How Would You Respond?

4.3 ABSTINENCE

Name ______________________________ Date ______________ Period ______

DIRECTIONS Write your responses.

1. Write an I-statement for each of these you-statements:
   - You walked to class with a friend who is very slow and you were late.
     You are so slow. It's your fault we're late!
   - You get a low grade on a test and your friend teases you about being stupid.
     I am not stupid, you are!
   - Your locker partner borrowed your math book and forgot to bring it back to school today.
     It is your fault I can't do my work because you forgot my book.

2. Write an I-statement for each of these situations:
   - You studied hard for the history test and passed with a good grade, but the teacher accused you of cheating.
   - It is your brother's turn to do the laundry, but he said he didn't have time to wash clothes yesterday. The outfit you wanted to wear to school is still dirty.
   - Your mom said you could go to your friend's party if you cleaned your room. You have a lot of homework and can't finish both things in time for the party.

3. Write your own situation and I-statement.

3 Steps

1. **State your *position.*** Say exactly what you mean:
   - "No, I don't want to do that."
   - "I would rather…"
   - "I believe that is…"

2. **Offer a *reason.*** Sometimes you may want to help others understand you better by explaining why:
   - "…because…"

3. **Recognize the other person's *feelings.*** Choose your words carefully to show you understand how others feel:
   - "…I imagine you feel…"
   - "…I can see how you'd feel…"

Practice for Assertiveness

1. You are standing in line to buy concert tickets and someone cuts in front of you.
2. Your brother or sister has borrowed your favorite sweater without permission.
3. Your friends want to go to an R-rated movie and you don't want to go.
4. Your parents are gone for the weekend so your boyfriend or girlfriend suggests spending the evening at your house.
5. Your boyfriend or girlfriend keeps trying to touch you too intimately.
6. Your boyfriend or girlfriend tells you that having sex will make you a real man or woman.
7. Your boyfriend or girlfriend says that if you were really in love you'd have sex together.
8. Your boyfriend or girlfriend tells you that it's OK to have sex because he or she will take care of everything.

Refusal Steps

1. **Ask questions.** Clarify what friends are asking you to do:
   - "Exactly what are you suggesting?"
   - "What would we do?"

2. **Name the trouble.** Say why you think this is a problem:
   - "There are too many risks for us now."
   - "That breaks the rules we made for ourselves."

3. **Identify the consequences.** Say what you think might happen if you do this:
   - "I/you could get pregnant."
   - "The risk of getting an STD is just too great."
   - "Our relationship is just not ready for this step yet. We could end up feeling really guilty and breaking up."

4. **Suggest alternatives.** Name other things you could do together:
   - "Instead of being alone, why don't we go to the movies?"
   - "Instead of being alone, why don't we go over to Julie's house?"

5. **Move on.** Walk away as you offer an alternative:
   - "If you change your mind, I'll be at Julie's. We can still go to the movie."

Refusing Under Pressure

If someone really pressures you:

- **Stop.** Look at the person directly and tell him or her to listen to you.
- **Stay calm.** Repeat what you said about the problem, consequences and alternatives.
- **Walk away.** Get away from the person and the situation.

The Story of Jamie and Lee

Jamie and Lee have been going out for 3 months. They are both seniors, looking forward to graduating from high school in 5 months. This is the first time either one has had a serious relationship. They are very happy together.

Together they made a decision to be abstinent because of all the possible negative consequences from being sexually intimate—the possibility of pregnancy or STD, guilt from going against their beliefs, stress on their relationship, etc. But lately it has been harder and harder to keep that decision.

They have just come from the homecoming dance. They get to Lee's house and find no one is home. Jamie suggests they sit together on the couch to talk. Lee isn't sure where that might lead.

Jamie and Lee

Name ______________________________ Date ______________ Period ______

Read **The Story of Jamie and Lee** and complete the dialogue so that each refusal step is shown. You may want to create several different dialogues for practice.

Step 1

Lee **asks questions:**

Step 2

Jamie doesn't see what the problem is, so Lee **names the trouble:**

Step 3

This doesn't stop Jamie from wanting to come in and spend time together, so Lee **identifies the consequences:**

Step 4

Jamie tells Lee not to worry and is still interested in coming in, so Lee **suggests alternatives:**

Step 5

When Jamie doesn't respond, Lee **moves on** by ______________________________ , and says:

Cartoon Dialog

Name ______________________ Date ______________ Period ________

Characters: ______________________

Relationship: ______________________

Situation: ______________________

Delay	**Question**
Trouble	**Consequences**
Alternatives	**Move on**

Delays and Refusals Cards

DIRECTIONS Copy and cut apart the steps to make cards. Make enough sets to have 1 card for each student. Try to have an equal number of each step.

Delay: Give yourself more time to respond.	**Identify the consequences:** Say what you think might happen if you do this.
Ask questions: Clarify what friends are asking you to do.	**Suggest alternatives:** Name other things you could do together.
Name the trouble: Say why you think this is a problem.	**Move on:** Walk away as you offer an alternative idea.

Saying No—Family and Student Page

This activity gives you an opportunity to practice saying no. Being able to say no when that is the right decision for you is an important skill.

Part 1

Use the **Refusal Steps** to respond to the following stories. Act out the story with the student as the person saying no and the adult as the other characters. Be sure to use each step of the skill.

Refusal Steps

1. Ask questions.
2. Name the trouble.
3. Identify the consequences.
4. Suggest alternatives.
5. Move on.

Story 1

Marie is out with some friends on Saturday night. It is 11:00 and her curfew is 11:30. Terry, who is driving the car, and the other kids want to go for pizza. To get Marie home in time, Terry would have to drive many miles out of the way, and the pizza place might be closed by the time they got back. Marie promised her parents she'd be home on time, and she feels it's important to keep her promise and their trust. What can Marie say to Terry and her other friends?

Story 2

Tony is new at school and wants to make friends. He is at a party with some kids from school who he thinks he would like as friends. He's a little nervous about making a good impression. Someone brings in some beer and is passing it around to everyone. Tony doesn't drink and he doesn't want to start because he promised his parents that he wouldn't. What can Tony say when he's offered a beer?

Story 3

Sue wants her boyfriend, Jake, to go back to her house after they've been to a romantic movie. Her family is gone for the weekend. Jake really likes Sue but is afraid that they might not be able to control themselves in this situation. What can he say to Sue?

(continued...)

Saying No—Family and Student Page

Continued

Story 4

Linda and Mike have been going out for several months. Mike wants to have sex but Linda doesn't. Since she really cares for Mike, how can she say no and not lose him as her boyfriend?

Part 2

Discuss how effective these skills might be in a real-life situation. Try trading places and have the adult use the refusal skills.

When you are finished, please complete the **Saying No—Feedback Form**, sign it and send it to school with your son or daughter as evidence of completion of the activity.

Saying No—Feedback Form

DIRECTIONS Your evaluation of this activity will help us as we work to bring families and the school closer together. Please respond to the following questions about this activity. Then sign the form and have your child return it to school as evidence of completion of the activity.

	very worthwhile				not at all worthwhile
Overall rating of this activity (circle one):	1	2	3	4	5

In what way was this activity worthwhile?

In what way was it *not* worthwhile?

Was any portion of this activity too difficult? How?

What suggestions do you have for improving this activity?

____________________	____________________	__________
Adult signature	Student signature	Date

Saying No in Words and Actions

Name ______________________________ Date ________________ Period ______

Develop a roleplay, using the characters of Jamie and Lee. Show the dialog between the 2 people. The dialog should realistically represent the conversation 2 people might have when discussing becoming sexually active.

Use stage direction comments to provide clues for nonverbal communication and good listening skills. Put them in parentheses.

The dialog should demonstrate the use of:

- I-statements
- assertiveness
- delay and refusal steps

Identify each of these in the dialog by highlighting the 3 skills in different colors or by using different markings—for example, underline I-statements, circle assertive statements and draw rectangles around delay and refusal steps. Some items may be marked as more than 1 skill.